FREEBIRD

WORK FREE. LIVE FREE.

RICK SHURTZ

SOUL
Tribe
PRESS

SoulTribe Press   Austin, Texas

Library of Congress Control Number 2014917212
ISBN 978-0-9907379-0-2
eISBN 978-0-9907379-1-9

First edition 2014
Printed in the United States of America

SoulTribe Press
www.soultribe.tv

For bulk orders, permission requests, and other inquiries, email
questions@soultribe.tv

This is a work of fiction. Names, characters, businesses, places, events and incidents are either the products of the author's imagination or used in a fictitious manner. Any resemblance to actual persons, living or dead, or actual events is purely coincidental.

Cover design: Betty Blake Churchill and M. Brady Clark
Interior design: Eric Jusino
Author photo: Lisa Hackbarth

To Johnny Gadado

Prelude

EVERYBODY works. The CEO runs a company, the stay-at-home parent runs a household, the teacher runs a classroom. It's been said that money makes the world go round. Maybe, but maybe not. Maybe work makes the world go round. If an individual doesn't work, the community suffers. If the community suffers, the nation suffers. If the nation suffers, the world suffers. Work matters. We all must do our part and do it well, but must we be miserable while doing it? Must we be enslaved? In the midst of life's reality—the reality of work—how might we be liberated? How might we be free?

Lola's

PART of the plan? Never. To say he surprised himself is to put it mildly. To say he shocked his colleagues misses the bull's-eye by a ring or two. Lose his job? Done. Lose future opportunities? Probably. Lose his friends? Not the friends he'd see tonight.

Tyler O'Brien slammed the car door and walked slowly across the dimly lit street. The night was crisp but not cold, his jacket just enough to do the job. Lola's, a local establishment frequented by a breadth of generations, sat a few blocks off the more common downtown scene. People went to Lola's *with* friends, not to find friends, which is why Tyler had been here the first Thursday of every month for several years now.

It took years to reconnect, but they eventually did so. They'd met in high school, went their own ways after graduation, but one by one slowly made their way back home. The Thursday ritual was initially unplanned but had become nearly sacred. The common bond between them was unique to other bonds in their lives. They had their work friends and the occasional neighbor, but this was different. This was the bond of history and time. They'd grown up together, which brought a kind of comfort that made their differences inconsequential.

Angie's laughter greeted Tyler as the door shut behind him. He cracked a smile and shook his head, knowing she was no doubt entertaining a semi-willing audience with a recent dramatic moment from her life, which was pretty much every moment for Angie. Doug—the political junkie of the group—saw Tyler first and welcomed him with a raised glass. The two had run track together years before as part of the same relay team.

"Angie went on a blind date," Doug pointed to an open chair. "He took our vegan friend to The Chop House." Tyler smiled lightly as he looked at a wide-eyed Angie, anxious to finish her story.

"Keep going," Tyler said while sitting down and signaling to their waitress to bring his preferred pint.

"So the waiter asks for my order, and I'm trying to figure out what to do. Do I go obnoxious, or do I just order a salad and pick around the cheese?"

Doug laughed. "Like either of us wonders which option you chose."

"You'd have been impressed by my self-control."

"So the carnivorous man must be good looking," Doug said.

Angie looked toward Doug. "Very. But that's not what..."

"Oh no! We've seen that look before. Don't tell me you like this guy. You're still seeing him, aren't you?"

A sly grin crossed Angie's face. "I think I'm in love."

"You've got to be kidding!" Doug's glass hit the table.

"You should have seen how he responded," Angie's eyes widened. "He was apologetic. He insisted on taking me somewhere else, which after his apology I didn't want him to do, but he did it anyway. He took me to a little market store. He bought all this stuff for a picnic we took to a park. He asked me all sorts of questions. He listened. He understood. By the end of the night we were laughing at the whole thing, and well," Angie paused, "we've seen a lot of each other since then."

Doug looked at Tyler. "How long? Do we track this on a stopwatch or a calendar?"

"I'll bring him next month. You'll love him."

"What's his name?" Tyler asked.

"Jack."

"Sounds like a meat-eater," Doug sneered. "Has he given up meat?"

"I wouldn't want him to do that for me. What he eats is his choice."

Doug and Tyler looked at each other and then back to Angie.

"Who are you, and where's Angie?" Doug said. "Either you're an impersonator, or Jack's a very rich man."

"Neither," Angie said. "Jack's an HR consultant and does well-enough, but he's no Tyler." Tyler raised his eyebrows but was accustomed to the shots. If anything, he liked being around a group of friends who could speak openly. They'd watched years ago when he started a software company with a college friend. While slugging their way through their first jobs out of college, they'd dreamed up a sales tracking system they knew could soar. With Tyler's drive it didn't take long for them to attract larger companies eager to acquire them. They held out as long as they could but finally sold when a company offered both cash and options. Tyler did well both in the sale and when the company went public, but he didn't have the money they thought he had. Much of it evaporated over the three and a half years he'd spent in Amsterdam.

Tyler quietly wondered if now was the time to break the news of recent events, but the moment quickly passed.

"Hey," the familiar voice of Blake Hill greeted them from behind. "Sounds like I missed another edition of *Angie's World*."

"Not really," Doug shook his head. "Just another chapter from the same old book."

"Not true!" Angie threw an elbow into Doug's side and turned to Blake, "How's our favorite doctor?"

"Bored." Blake pointed to his selection from the list of seasonal drafts.

Blake hated being a suburban doctor—hated the hours, hated insurance companies. They all remembered the night years ago lying on blankets at the end of a nearby runway, watching airplanes land, and dreaming of their futures. Blake's dream was the most noble. He'd go to med school, move to a third-world country, and open a free clinic for people who really needed it. School debt kept him back the first few years.

"Has 'the patient' come back?" Doug asked.

Blake's eyes brightened. For three months he'd given updates on an outrageously beautiful patient who was either a hypochondriac or was suffering from an acute desire to gain the doctor's affection.

"Twice," Blake said.

"She's into you Dr. Hill. Why don't you ask her out?" Angie had a way of asking the question on everybody's mind.

"Maybe I did."

"You didn't!" Angie smacked the table. Last month Blake was concerned about crossing an ethical line since she was his patient. Doug had chided him for being a stringent rule-follower.

"I did."

"How? What'd you do?" Angie wanted details.

Blake paused, reveling a bit in this uncommon development, "I wrote her a prescription."

The table went silent and all eyes were on Blake.

"What do you mean *you wrote her a prescription*?" Doug asked slowly.

"She came in two days ago asking to review the cholesterol test we ran the week before. I'd already had a nurse call her saying her numbers were good enough, but she came in anyway asking how to get her numbers even better. We got talking about exercise, and I wrote her a prescription."

"And what did you prescribe?" Doug said.

Blake took a drink and set his glass down. "She had this smile on her face. Actually, we were both smiling, almost laughing. It was one of those moments when the game is being played, both people know it and know the other person knows it as well. So I pulled out my prescription pad and told her I knew exactly what would help."

"Which was?" Angie couldn't contain herself.

"Saturday, 9:00 a.m., hike Deer Creek with Blake Hill."

The group was stunned. Angie clapped. Tyler nodded silently with approval. Doug raised his glass, "This is a moment we must mark."

They gave a collective nod and raised their glasses.

All eyes instinctively went to Doug, who had a way with words. "So Angie's in love with a meat-eater and Blake tells us he's broken a rule and gotten a date in the same instant." Doug placed a hand on Blake's shoulder. "On this historic night, we drink in honor of hell freezing over."

The group laughed and clashed glasses.

As the glasses came back to the table Blake spoke up, "But I do have one small problem."

"Here we go," Doug leaned back, shaking his head.

"It's not what you think. The date's on. I'm going." Blake set his drink on a napkin. "The problem is I made the date without thinking. I'm double-booked."

"That's easy," Doug said. "Cancel the conflict. I don't care if you're meeting with the president. You're going on this date."

"I'm going on the date, but the conflict is mildly sensitive. I've canceled on this guy two times. I don't want to cancel again."

"Who is he?" Doug was in problem-solving mode.

"He's a friend of my parents. They think he'll help me sort through my disdain for the suburban doctor gig."

"Some sort of career-counseling-shrink?" Angie asked.

"No, a minister."

"Cancel it," Tyler spoke nearly for the first time.

"Actually," Blake said, "I had another idea." Taking a deep breath, Blake turned to Tyler, "And it involves you."

Tyler raised his eyebrows but didn't respond.

"The meeting is not a meeting," Blake said. "I'm supposed to play golf with the guy. I hate golf. Didn't you play golf in high school, Tyler?"

Blake took a drink, giving time for this seed of a thought to germinate.

Doug answered for Tyler. "He played three years. Last time he played he got suspended for playing drunk in one of the tournaments. Then our extremely talented but painfully stubborn friend never went back, even though the coach said he was good enough to win state."

"I hate golf." Tyler lied. They didn't know it, but he'd recently picked it up again for the sole purpose of slamming a colleague he despised, which at a hundred bucks a hole netted an easy four hundred dollar gain. Regardless, he saw where this was going and wanted none of it. No way would he play a round of golf with a minister. The last minister he'd talked to had officiated his sister's wedding. Reverend Longwind had nothing to say but clearly loved the sound of his own voice. The man had a talent for crafting long sentences that communicated absolutely nothing. The only person who hung on his every word was his sister's new mother-in-law. No surprises there.

"This man has never met me. He doesn't know what I look like. All you have to do is show up and be me." Blake then played his trump card. "Don't think of it as a favor. Think of it as a dare."

Nobody said anything. Blake had positioned this well. He'd mellowed a bit in recent years, but Tyler had always lived on the edge. In younger years he'd never pass on a dare, especially if it could make for a good story.

"No," Tyler said, "I'd play golf for you, but not with a minister. I can't spend that long with a guy who's going to pray over his shots and try to baptize me in a water hazard."

Angie was shocked. "Tyler O'Brien is going to pass on a dare? Is this the same Tyler who streaked the dance club on our senior spring break trip to Mexico? Is this the same Tyler who parachutes and hang glides? You mean to tell me you'll ride a motorcycle through Europe, climb some mountain on the other side of the globe, and smoke who knows what with some of the shadiest characters in Amsterdam, but you won't play a single round of golf with a minister? It's taken a while, but I think we've finally found something you won't do."

"I don't know where my clubs are." It wasn't really a lie. He wasn't sure if his clubs were in his trunk or in the garage.

"I've got twenty bucks that says you'll do it, and you'll win." Angie reached for her purse knowing Tyler's weakness for a bet.

Doug pulled out his wallet and dropped two twenties on the table. "I'm in. You don't even have to beat the guy. Just channel Blake and play."

Blake looked at Tyler while placing a hundred and fifty dollars on the table. "That's enough for your greens fee and drinks when you're done. Just don't drink before you play. You don't want to get suspended again."

Tyler closed his eyes and shook his head. Silently, he wondered what eighteen holes with a minister would be like. His mind then jumped to the recent events his friends knew nothing about. He really didn't want to do this, but it wasn't like he had anything better to do. It *would* make for a decent story, and he'd never passed on a dare, especially for two hundred and ten dollars.

Slowly, Tyler leaned over, put his arms around the cash, and dragged it back as if he'd won a hand of poker.

"Game on!" Doug shouted and raised his freshly served glass for a second toast.

The First Hole

TYLER slammed the door and walked to the back of his car where the trunk was already open. He'd yet to give much thought to how he'd be Blake, but did it really matter? His golfing partner didn't know Blake. Tyler could be whomever he wanted to be, which led to the few ideas he did have.

Despite his resistance, Tyler had made peace with the day on two accounts. For starters, he'd concocted a couple of Blake stories to lay on the guy. No doubt the stories would make their way back to Blake's family in record time. At first he thought he'd tell the minister he was gay, that he had hidden it from his parents for years, and that he wanted his advice. He loved the idea initially, but the thought of eighteen awkward holes with Reverend Homophobe lost its charm after a while. He had a few other ideas that wouldn't ruin the morning, which reflected his second reason for a partially changed disposition.

Tyler was looking for escape.   Recent events had brought about a change he never anticipated, never sought, and certainly never wanted. But it was done, and today he'd do what he should have done weeks ago. "Greens fees aren't cheap," he muttered to himself while rifling through his trunk looking for his golf shoes, "but they're cheaper than counseling." If he had to play, he hoped to play slowly with a few laughs at Blake's expense. It had been a long time since he'd done anything slowly. Even longer since he'd laughed.

Tyler felt his phone vibrate in his pocket. Already, Doug had texted him a mock medical question about testicular cancer, Angie had texted a joke about a doctor and a minister playing golf together, and Blake had sent a selfie of him and his "patient" smiling broadly. He'd yet to respond to any of them.

Tyler fumbled for his phone and found another text from Blake.

You there yet?

Struck by his opportunity, Tyler responded before lacing his second shoe.

There yet? I thought you said next Saturday!

He attached a recent photo of himself unshaven and drinking coffee on his back patio.

Finished with his shoes, Tyler picked up his bag, and made his way to the clubhouse.

The clubhouse was simple. There was a small pro shop with a bar and grill called The 19th Hole. He thought he might enjoy a few drinks when his game was done.

"Are you Dr. Hill?" asked the man behind the counter.

"I am," Tyler said. A quick glance around the room revealed only one other person, a gal facing a rack of women's clothing.

"Your greens fee's been paid. Ned's warming up at the first tee."

Tyler turned to the door. He certainly didn't expect that. He had no use for preacher-types, but that didn't mean he'd want the guy's money. As he walked toward the first tee he quietly wondered if this minister might be attempting to make Blake feel indebted to him. Maybe he was angling for a contribution to his church.

Tyler walked a gentle curving path toward the first tee. He'd hoped for a little time at the driving range, but he'd slept later than planned. As he turned the corner in view of the minister, Tyler's phone vibrated with another text.

Seriously?!

Blake wasn't naïve, but Tyler knew the photo was convincing. He'd taken it a couple weeks back when one of his direct reports, the VP of Sales, texted him to tell him the Chairman of the Board had made an appearance in the office that morning. The expression on his face in the photo was a dumbfounded "What do you want me to do?" look. It was the perfect picture to send Blake.

Tyler quickly texted back.

I'll get there as quick as I can.

Tyler approached the first tee as the minister was taking a few practice swings. The man wore a comfortable looking hat and stood club-length from his sun-bleached bag. He gave Tyler a gentle nod. "Here we go," Tyler thought to himself, "I'm Blake Hill, suburban doctor."

"Blake Hill." A hand was extended and received.

"Ned Peterson." The man's grip was firm and confident.

"Thanks for picking up the greens fee. You didn't have to do that."

"Glad you made it."

Tyler was silent expecting the man to speak up. Instead, the minister walked quietly to his bag.

"My parents speak highly of you, Reverend Peterson." Tyler knew little of the Hills' opinions, but he figured he was on safe ground. After drinks at Lola's, Blake explained that his parents started attending Reverend Peterson's church in recent years. It was a bit odd. Blake's family didn't attend church when they were all in high school.

"Please, call me Ned."

Tyler nodded as Ned pulled a fresh ball from his bag. The man wasn't old but was certainly weathered. He exuded a quiet confidence—or was it smugness—that Tyler noticed immediately?

"Have you played this course?" Tyler asked as his phone vibrated from another text.

"Many times. I've much to learn from it though."

Tyler lifted his phone from his pocket.

"How are your parents?" Ned placed a ball on the tee.

Tyler looked at his phone.

"They're doing great. Looks like Dad just sent me a text."

The text was from Angie.

> *Blake just texted me. Did you seriously think it was next week?!!!*

"Nice," Tyler whispered to himself. "Dad's text says you're quite the golfer."

Ned looked up from his practice swing. "I called your dad last night to see if he'd join us. Said he had to work today. Tell him he needs to break out of the office and catch us on the back nine."

Tyler quietly imagined the meltdown had he shown up this morning and found Mr. Hill standing next to Ned. "You know my dad, we'll never get him away from the office. Even on a Saturday."

Tyler turned his phone toward Ned who was stretching with a few slow practice swings. Quietly, he snapped a picture. Ned heard the fake camera shutter and turned Tyler's way.

"Thought I'd send him a photo to see if we can entice him away."

Tyler attached the photo of Ned to his text to Angie.

Not a word to Blake.

"Mind if I tee off?" Ned asked.

"He who pays gets honors."

Ned took one more practice swing and positioned himself to play. His drive was exactly what Tyler expected after knowing the man mere minutes—the ball traveled a modest but respectable distance and landed in the middle of the fairway.

"Nice shot." Tyler really didn't care, but it was good to know he'd be playing with a man who knew how to handle his clubs.

Ned stepped back. Tyler pulled his driver from the bag. In high school he joked that his driver cost less than a girlfriend and treated him better. Somewhere along the way he gave it a name.

"Ned, meet Sally."

Ned cracked a gentle smile, "Sally, huh?"

"She wasn't cheap, but at a hundred bucks a hole against the Sunday morning boys, she was worth every penny."

It was the beginning of one of Tyler's concocted stories on Blake. He'd mentally written an elaborate script of Blake's gambling habits, playing while his parents sat in this man's church, losing everything he'd made as a doctor on quick trips to Vegas, and still drowning in debt from medical school.

"Back in the day I had a similar group. We were all young and broke, though, so we'd play a dollar a hole or for beer money."

Tyler paused as he placed his ball, a bit surprised by the minister's response.

Tyler's drive was long. He raised his hand to shade his eyes in hopes of tracking his ball. It peaked right where he hoped it would drop but sliced mildly to the right.

"Come back, come back," he quietly whispered.

The fairway was broad, more than compensating for his slice. Tyler made a note for adjustments to his stance on the next drive.

Without comment, they grabbed their bags and began walking as Tyler's phone vibrated from another text.

The Second Hole

THE text was from Angie.

Ha!!! You're evil, but I love it. Blake's flipping out.

Tyler put his phone back in his pocket, quietly smiling at the thought of Blake sweating bullets. He'd put him out of his misery before too long. As they walked toward the second tee, Tyler couldn't help but enjoy his unemployed status. He was playing golf and laughing with friends. He'd missed this.

"Never again," he thought.

Both men played well on the first hole. Ned was twenty-five yards off the green in two, on the green in three, and in the hole in four. Tyler was off to a good—albeit a little rusty—start as well. His second shot landed on the far side of the green. He nearly two-putted, but his second putt ringed the hole leading to a quick tap for one over par.

"Not bad for a preacher," Tyler said as they made their way to the second tee.

Ned pulled his driver as he walked. "First you call me Reverend. Now you call me a preacher."

"Isn't that what you do?"

The two men walked past a collection of bushes and turned toward the next tee.

"I preach, but not in the way most people think of preaching."

They set their bags by a bench beside the tee box.

"Preaching, as most have come to expect it, is why a group of guys spend their Sunday mornings on a golf course playing for a hundred bucks a hole, and quite frankly, I don't blame them."

Tyler smiled.

"Preaching is also why I didn't set foot in a church for the better part of twelve years."

Tyler offered a curious look but didn't ask.

Ned placed a tee in the ground, positioned himself, and drove the ball a hundred and fifty yards out where the fairway doglegged to the left. As he placed his driver in his bag, Ned broke the silence, "The green's just fifty yards around that bend. No need to attempt anything heroic."

Tyler positioned his ball on the tee, and placed his drive fifteen yards beyond Ned's.

They grabbed their bags and began walking.

"If you don't preach, what do you do?" Tyler really wasn't interested, but had strategically planned to keep the conversation off himself early in the game.

"It's not that I don't preach. I do preach and believe deeply in what I do. But I don't do what most people think of when they think of preaching."

Tyler considered asking Ned why he left the church for twelve years. He wasn't sure he really wanted to know, though, and missed his chance in the worst way.

"So you're a doctor, what kind?"

Tyler thought for a moment and was surprised that he honestly didn't know the answer. How could he not know about Blake's practice? A brief thought about the out-of-touch leadership he'd been under and how it had robbed him of life passed through his mind. "Internal medicine," he answered.

It sounded vague enough and sophisticated enough that he instinctively thought it would work. The moment he said it, though, he knew he'd have to change the subject quickly. He knew absolutely nothing about internal medicine. He didn't even know what a doctor specializing in internal medicine did or if that was specific enough to satisfy the question.

"Is that right?" Ned said.

He didn't want to be abrupt, but sensing a follow-up question from Ned, Tyler said, "Yes, I'm here to get away from it, though. I did three surgeries yesterday. I can't think about it."

Ned's walk slowed. "That's interesting."

"No, not really. You get a little sick of it after a few years."

Ned nodded slowly. With his head cocked, he looked directly at Tyler. "Isn't that something," he finally said and continued his walk down the fairway.

The remainder of the hole was played in silence. Tyler shot par. Ned was one over. The game was tied.

The Third Hole

As the two men approached the third tee, Tyler's phone rang. Knowing it was undoubtedly Blake, he lifted his phone from his pocket.

"It's my dad," Tyler said.

Ned nodded giving unspoken approval to interrupt their game.

"Good morning." Tyler answered the phone.

"I can't believe you screwed this up."

"Wish you were here, Dad. The perfect morning for golf."

There was a long silence on the line.

"Oh you've got to be kidding me."

"We just finished the second hole. Ned's a solid golfer. Much better than you said." Tyler smiled as he looked toward Ned.

"I just got off the phone with Doug," Blake said. "He's on his way to cover for you covering for me."

Tyler laughed. "No, we don't need your coaching, Dad. We're doing just fine on our own. Wish you could have joined us, though. Maybe another time."

"Unbelievable," Blake said as the phone went dead.

"Alright, Dad. Don't work too hard. I'll talk to you later today and give you the update."

Tyler smiled at the thought of next month's Lola's gathering as he placed his phone back in his pocket and quickly brought the conversation back to golf, "Tell me about this hole."

"It's a par five. Long and straight. No gimmicks."

Tyler placed his ball, stepped up, and swung his club with resolve. His drive was long but landed in the rough just behind a mid-fairway sand trap. A string of colorful words pierced the air.

Ned's drive was shorter than Tyler's and landed slightly in the rough on the other side of the fairway.

"Looks like we're off to a rough start on this one," Ned said as they picked up their bags.

"My apologies for the language." Tyler wasn't truly apologetic, but it seemed like something Blake would say, even though it didn't really matter what Blake would say.

"You be you, Blake. I'll be me."

Tyler couldn't help but smile at the irony of Ned's statement.

Looking for a way to keep the conversation off himself, Tyler asked, "So tell me, why'd you leave the church for twelve years?"

Ned didn't respond immediately.

"Last time I told that story it sparked a conversation that took us all the way to lunch at the nineteenth hole."

Tyler welcomed the idea of a long story about something other than Blake's medical practice, but he didn't like the idea of it turning into a conversation. There was no backing out now, though.

"All we've got is time."

Ned lifted his hat briefly wiping his brow. The morning was cool with a light breeze, but the rising sun was making its presence known.

"Have you ever snapped?" Ned finally asked.

"Snapped?" Snapping was a good enough descriptor for what had just happened in his life, but he couldn't talk about that. "I think you just saw me snap after my last shot."

"No, not that," Ned said. "That was frustration. By snapping, I mean have you ever had the pressure build up so intensely that in an instant you became undone?"

Images of last week's banquet passed through Tyler's mind. He was simultaneously proud and a bit embarrassed. No regrets, though. He was moving forward. "I don't think I have," he finally said, "I'm pretty laid back." The question, though, peaked his curiosity for Ned's story. Tyler noted a mild conflict rising within him. He wasn't about to back off his plan of a few laughs at Blake's expense, but Ned had caught him a bit by surprise—more likable than he'd expected.

The two men walked down the fairway toward Ned's ball.

"I was a young man. My formative years were spent here, but I'd moved to Chicago looking to make my fortune in business. It was adventurous and exciting at first. I was far from home and far from most anything familiar. I'd grown up going to church, so after a few months of living there I was looking for a taste of familiarity and made my way to a local church. It was the only thing that felt anything like home."

"Am I really interested in this guy's story?" Tyler thought to himself. He pushed away his interest, determined to wait out the story and get back to Blake's gambling problems.

"My work started out strong. I did fairly well. I worked for a company selling long-term leases on heavy equipment. But then the wind shifted, as the wind often does, and I couldn't get a sale to save my life. My boss was leaning hard on my back. My counterpart, a guy who sold exactly what I sold but in a different territory, scored a couple deals that were great for him but only highlighted my lack of effectiveness. So my stock, so to speak, was low and sinking lower. I was determined, though, and for a good six months I worked tirelessly, day and night. I wanted to be effective, but I was also putting on a show for my overbearing boss. He came into his position from another company where he'd done fairly well, but I discovered when working a trade show with him that he couldn't sell at all. He couldn't explain our equipment, and didn't have a clue how to differentiate us from our competition. So it was the perfect storm of misery. I'm working for a guy I don't respect, my counterpart is performing, I'm failing and failing miserably, and I have absolutely no life outside of work. It was miserable."

Tyler's curiosity reluctantly rose once again. Parallels to his own life abounded.

"So there I am, struggling to carve a life out for myself, and I'm keeping up my habit of going to church. At first, I liked the preacher, and he was most certainly what you think of when you think of a preacher. He spoke with authority. He made it sound like he really knew what he was talking about, which did something for me. I was increasingly insecure and got a charge out of feeling 'right.' Over time, though, something began to happen in me. I couldn't identify it at the time; I hadn't done enough living or surrounded myself with people of genuine wisdom, and I was too proud and too foolish to ask for help. Looking back, the best way I can describe my condition is to say my soul was shriveling up. I was lonely. I was tired. I was working harder than I had ever worked in my life, and it wasn't going well. I didn't have friends, just acquaintances. And honestly, I wouldn't have admitted this then, but I was scared."

Ned stopped talking briefly while locating his ball. He rested his bag and pulled out his three wood as the two men looked left and right over a small area between two trees. Tyler pointed to the ball.

"It was a low point, the lowest I'd ever been. I come from a hardworking family that didn't show emotion. That's the way you did things back then. You sucked it up, gutted it out, and never let on you might be struggling. I'd never known anyone to feel how I felt."

Ned's shot drifted high and bounced to a stop forty yards shy of the green. Tyler had yet to find a three wood that treated him as well as Sally, but he pulled out what he had as the two men walked toward his ball.

"My struggle heightened my awareness at church. I was searching. I needed help. Like I said, the preacher seemed to know what he was talking about, so I was all ears."

"Do you any good?" Tyler's question surprised himself. He didn't care if it did him any good.

Ned shook his head. "Everything the man said was 'out there' and not 'in here,'" Ned pointed to his heart. "It was all about the problems in the world. He'd beat up on one problem in the world and then beat up on another. I didn't realize it at the time, but most of it was political stuff. He was always up in arms about some law or lack of law. Not exactly the kind of teaching that does much of anything for a shriveled up soul."

The course, surprisingly quiet for a Saturday, encouraged the lingering story. Neither man rushed the game or the conversation, and Tyler—despite his irritation with his own interest—was genuinely curious to know what Ned's "snapping" looked like.

"So what happened?"

Ned shook his head. "Let's just say there came a day when I didn't let him get away with it."

Ned paused as Tyler lined up for his shot. His ball bounced and rolled to the right side of the fairway about 20 yards from the green.

"It was a mid-summer Sunday morning. I was a mess inside. All my wires were crossed. I made my way to church in hope of help. I sat down on the right side. I could take you to the exact spot. When it came time for the preaching, the man pulled out all the stops. Earlier that week he'd read an editorial from some newspaper I'd never heard of. Some guy two states away had written about why he believed posting the Ten Commandments in public schools was unconstitutional. You'd have thought that preacher had seen a ghost. He was in shock. He started with the founding fathers, made his way through the freedoms defended in all the wars, and ended by leading the congregation through a rousing rendition of *Onward Christian Soldiers*."

Ned raised his eyebrows and shook his head.

"So there I was, listening to this man rant and rave about something that did absolutely nothing for my shriveled up soul. He was worked up like I'd never seen him. His passion and authority that had originally grabbed my attention was in full force that day. But my insides were screaming, and out of the corner of my eye, I noticed something I'd never stopped to consider until that moment."

Ned looked toward Tyler.

"The walls on both sides of the sanctuary were empty."

Whatever Ned noticed about empty walls was lost on Tyler. The lack of response on Tyler's face was evident, so Ned continued.

"This man was all cranked up about posting the Ten Commandments in public places, and yet the Ten Commandments weren't posted in the one place you might expect them to be posted if posting them was truly that important." Ned's face was alive with passion.

"My mind got to thinking. I'd been involved in that church. I'd been in every room countless times. I had never, not once, seen a posting of the Ten Commandments. Even more, I had never, not once, heard that preacher give any instruction on the Ten Commandments. Now there's nothing that says churches must post the Ten Commandments, and I was no expert on constitutional law. I had no idea what I thought about posting or not posting the Ten Commandments in public places. But I knew one thing for certain. If this man had such deep convictions about posting the Ten Commandments in public places, then why had he never posted them in his church? Why had he never given a single lesson on the meaning of the Ten Commandments? Why was it that the only time I'd ever heard the Ten Commandments mentioned was over a political issue that did absolutely nothing for me, and failed to even address the content of the Ten Commandments?"

Ned stopped, pulled out his pitching wedge, and lined up for his shot. His ball landed in a sand trap on the far side of the green.

Tyler walked to his own ball and placed it on the green.

"So what'd you do?" Tyler asked.

"I helped end the service. After singing the final stanza of *Onward Christian Soldiers* the preacher launched into his closing prayer. He was going on and on. The man could not give a simple prayer. He finally got to the point where you could tell he was on descent, had the landing gear down, and was lining up for the runway. He was giving his, 'In the name of the Father, Son, and Holy Ghost' line, but this alone could take an additional half minute or more. He packed each statement with endless descriptions."

Ned cracked a smile.

"And then it happened. I snapped. I couldn't help myself. I wrapped his prayer up for him."

"You did what?"

"I wrapped it up for him. He had just finished saying something like 'In the name of the glorious Father who is sovereign over all, who created all we see and know and touch, who loves us and who is all-powerful, all-knowing, and all-present.' He was getting ready to move into 'and in the name of the Son who...' and that's when I snapped."

"What'd you do?"

"I blurted, 'In the name of the Son and of the Holy Spirit. Amen!'"

Tyler laughed, "What happened?"

"The preacher was so surprised by my words that it actually worked. He shut his trap, the organ kicked in, and he made his procession to the back door to greet people as they left. Every eye in that sanctuary was on me, and you'd think I'd be embarrassed. Not at all. Not even close. I was so fed up with that man that I stepped right out in that aisle and followed him, lockstep, to the door."

By this time Ned was standing in the middle of the sand trap. Tyler stood beside him near the edge of the green but out of the way.

"So there we were, standing by the back door, and I walked straight up to him, nose to nose and said, 'Sir, I have a question for you.' He was still a bit flustered and confused on how the service ended.

"'Okay, what's your question?' he asked.

"I said, 'You obviously are very passionate about the Ten Commandments being posted in public places, but I can't help but notice you don't have them posted anywhere in this church. I've never heard you mention the Ten Commandments before today, and to be truthful, you didn't talk about the content of the Ten Commandments. You talked about public policy. It got me thinking. Do you really know the Ten Commandments?'

"He shot back, 'Do I know the Ten Commandments?'

"I kept on, 'That's right. Do you know them?'

"Of course he thought he knew them, and no doubt he was very familiar with them, but I was genuinely unconvinced he knew them well enough to name them. 'If you know them…name them,' I said.

"His forehead wrinkled, 'Name them?'

"'That's right,' I said. 'Name the Ten Commandments.'

"I don't think that man had ever been challenged in his life. The entire congregation listened in utter silence. He paused, and barreled back, 'Are you suggesting I don't know my Bible?'

"'I tell you what.' I said. 'Don't feel like you have to name all ten. Just name the first five.'

"He stood quietly and didn't say a word. The room was silent. During his sermon-rant I'd looked up the Ten Commandments, so I had them fresh in my mind. Finally, after a good ten seconds I turned to the congregation. 'Anyone? What are the first five commandments?'

"There was a long pause. I looked from face to face. Finally someone called out, 'Thou shalt not murder.'

"'Wrong,' I said. 'That's number six.'

"I walked out of that church and never looked back. Within a few hours I was both relieved and surprised by what I'd done. I didn't regret it. I just surprised myself."

Tyler walked to his ball after Ned hit his from the trap to about five feet from the pin. Tyler two-putted and closed out the hole with par. Ned did the same on the green but was one over.

They grabbed their bags and began to walk to the fourth tee.

"But now you're a preacher or minister or whatever you want to call it. You didn't walk away for good. What happened?"

"Like I said, I was away for twelve years. I'll never regret walking away from that church, but the next twelve years were extremely hard."

Ned wiped his hands with a towel dangling from the top of his bag.

"The day after snapping, I resigned from my job. I offered two weeks of service, but my boss didn't want it. We both knew I needed out of that job. I hadn't had the courage to quit, and he hadn't had the courage to fire me. I went to my apartment, packed my belongings and drove home. It was good to be on familiar turf but things had changed. I couldn't get a direction and didn't know what to do. It took a while."

"How so?"

"It took a while to discover what it was I needed to discover. I spun through job after job. I had a few serious girlfriends. Nothing stuck. Jobs didn't stick. Girls would come and go. I was a mess and only got messier."

That comment, "It took a while to discover what it was I needed to discover," got Tyler's attention, but his interest irritated him. Other than the church aspects, Ned's story sounded dangerously familiar to his own, which made him wonder, what had he discovered? Tyler had other ideas for their conversation, though. How could he glean a bit of this guy's experience but lay out at least one of the stories he'd concocted about Blake. The thought surprised him. Was he really interested? Not at all.

The tee for the fourth hole sat fifty yards from the parking lot. Tyler placed his bag next to a ball cleaner and out of the corner of his eye noticed a man at the back of his car angrily throwing golf shoes into the trunk.

It was Doug.

The Fourth Hole

DOUG slammed his trunk shut and stopped abruptly when he turned toward the driver's side of the car and saw Tyler.

Tyler smiled, raising his arm to wave.

Doug, with a sly smile, gently shook his head. After an unusually long gaze between them, Doug waved back, but with just one of his five fingers.

Tyler turned toward Ned to see if he'd noticed. He had.

"Friend of yours?" Ned asked with a smile.

Tyler saw his opportunity. "Yes, I've known him since high school. Unfortunately, I owe him money."

Tyler dropped a ball and lined up facing Doug's car, a high-mileage beater he knew Doug didn't care about.

"We hit Vegas together a couple months back. It didn't go well for me. He had to cover."

Ned offered a gentle laugh while pulling his driver from his bag. "We should introduce your high school friends to my high school friends. I suspect they'd get along great."

As Doug's car backed out of its parking space, Tyler's ball bounced off its hood.

"Nice shot," Ned said.

Tyler placed his pitching wedge back in his bag. "You ever been to Vegas?"

"A couple times, years ago," Ned said, "but I gave it up after losing nearly three thousand dollars in record time. Decided I'd never go back."

"Good call," Tyler said. "That last trip took its toll. Hoping I can make it up when I go again in two weeks. I suppose I shouldn't admit that to you, though."

"Remember, Blake, you be you. I'll be me."

Tyler nodded, struck again by the unknown irony of the statement.

Tyler looked toward Ned. "I've got a plan to regain my losses. I've been studying card counting."

"Is that right?" Ned said.

Tyler expected Ned to say more, something about the foolishness of gambling or the evils of Las Vegas, but he didn't. He saw passing curiosity in his eyes, but Ned seemed to let it go.

Tyler lined up for his drive. He felt better having spiced things up a bit, but was surprised by his next thought. He wanted to ask Ned about the wisdom he'd discovered. He pushed the thought away and focused on his drive.

The fourth hole had water. It was lined with trees on the far side and had a large fountain in the middle. To a non-golfer it was a scenic lake. To a golfer the lake was a ball magnet. The water didn't need to interfere but had a way of doing so.

Tyler's drive eclipsed the lake and rolled to a stop about three quarters of the way down the fairway. It was his cleanest drive of the day. Ned's drive landed in the center of the fairway, just past a midway sand trap.

As they walked, Tyler again thought Ned might ask about his gambling problem. It seemed like the perfect opportunity for a minister to launch into something, but Ned didn't do it.

As they neared Ned's ball, Tyler surprised himself.

"So tell me a bit about this wisdom you came into." As he said it, Tyler wondered where this might lead. He was genuinely curious, though, and Angie's comments about being willing to do anything other than golf with a minister rang through his mind. He'd taken many risks in life, why not risk a little here? If things went south, he could take whatever this guy dished out. It might even make for a better story.

Ned didn't respond as he pulled his three wood and walked toward his ball. Finally, after placing his bag down, he said, "To best understand the wisdom I came into—if you really want to hear it—you need to hear about a man named Jackson Powell and the advice he gave me. It needs a bit more context, though."

Ned went silent as he lined up for his shot. His ball grazed a second collection of trees and rolled pitching distance from the green. The two men walked toward Tyler's ball.

"I was the first in my family to graduate from college. My parents were proud; I was invincible. That first job selling long-term leases was like being teed up with the wind at my back. I was going to set records and carve out a life for me and my future family. Snapping was good for me. It gave me a fresh start. I rolled into town and was more than just physically back; I was back emotionally. I had done enough losing and was ready to rack up a few points."

Tyler anticipated what was coming next, "Let me guess, the points didn't rack up like you thought they would."

Ned nodded. "That's right. I'd gain a little traction and slip. I'd try something else and slip again. You're talking about a hardworking, responsible young man. I had lazy friends who lacked direction. They just weren't trying and made a life out of blaming others for their lack of success. That wasn't me. I worked hard. I fought. I applied every ounce of mental and physical strength I could muster. I'd get a few wins here and there, but the biggest thing I got was tired. Even more, I was confused. I was playing by the rules. I was doing what everyone told me to do, and I was still losing. And that was just my work life. My relational life wasn't much better. I dated around but either I was interested and they weren't, or they were interested and I wasn't. I had my heart set on a gal I'd grown up with. She ended up with a young attorney who had just landed his dream job. It was salt on a wound."

"What'd you do?" Despite his inhibitions, Tyler enjoyed a good story, and Ned seemed to enjoy telling them. He hadn't expected a guy who had any experience or interest in business. He'd expected an out-of-touch blowhard. Maybe he could just keep this guy telling stories—it might even be interesting—and then throw in an occasional shot at Blake to make for a better story of his own.

"I sunk. You wouldn't have known it by casual conversation, but I was in a tough spot. Even more, all I wanted to do was quit trying. I'd read books on how to be successful, and I'd done the things they taught. It just wasn't working."

Tyler set down his bag and pulled out his five iron.

"Did you ever catch a break?" Tyler asked as he lined up for his shot. Ned waited to answer as Tyler's ball arched and then bounced on the green but well past the hole.

"I'd nearly given up. Actually, I had given up but was still going through the motions externally, and then I caught a break."

Tyler smiled, happy for the young man, now aged, walking beside him.

"Through an uncle or cousin—some guy I'd barely met—I landed a job selling commercial real estate. I threw myself at it and nobody was more surprised than me to see that it worked. It didn't take long to figure out I could make a pile of money. By this time it had been about two years since I'd moved home. The next couple of years went so fast it's a blur. Before long I left the original firm and started my own. I was hitting on all eight cylinders. That's when I met the love of my life. She was, and still is, a gem. We met through a mutual friend and were married eight months later." Ned paused to reflect.

"You have no idea what I've put her through."

Tyler nodded. He'd yet to marry, but he'd come close a few years back. As they walked Tyler considered his relational world. Doug, Angie, and the rest were the tried and true. He'd know them the rest of his life and wouldn't trade them for anything. But he wondered what it would be like to have someone to ride life's ups and downs with as Ned described—a soul mate. Recent years at work had been so intense there had been no hope of relationships of any depth. Now he was abruptly on the other extreme. He had plenty of time but knew his life lacked the kind of stability a committed relationship would want.

Ned pulled his pitching wedge and swung it by his side as he neared his ball. The conversation went silent as he lined up for his shot, which bounced and then rolled about ten yards from the pin. They both pulled their putters and made their way to the green.

"I was on a roll for about eight years. It was fantastic. I brokered deals and ultimately owned several properties of my own. I made a pile of money and had a great time doing it."

Ned paused.

"Then it happened,"

"What happened?"

"It crashed."

"What crashed?"

"My business. It crashed so hard seismologists could have measured it on the Richter scale."

Tyler couldn't help but chuckle and shake his head. "I bet I know how it happened."

Tyler's putt ringed the hole. He grimaced as it rolled three feet downhill.

"This one's pretty obvious," Ned agreed.

Tyler took a shot at finishing the story while Ned eyed the green planning his putt. "You felt invincible and overextended your credit. A project or two didn't go according to plan. Maybe you lost a major tenant. In a matter of weeks bankers were breathing down your neck."

"That's close enough, but don't stop there. I went from the big house on Oak Street to the Court House on Main Street in record time. Eventually I filed for bankruptcy. I didn't want to do it. Every fiber in my body revolted, but I had to. I'd lost it all. The courts didn't demand I sell my house, but I couldn't sit on it when I owed real people real money. My wife and I, along with our firstborn, moved into a small apartment. I couldn't believe it. I thought I'd left that kind of struggle long behind."

Ned's putt dropped in the hole. Tyler lined up for his short putt and finished out the hole.

"You use whiteboards much as a doctor?"

"Whiteboards?" Tyler spent more time in front of a whiteboard, leading teams in his company, than he spent doing most anything else. "Every now and then. Not too much, though. Quite a bit during my residency."

Ned walked over toward a sand trap. "Pretend for a moment this sand is a whiteboard." With his putter, Ned etched a triangle in the sand. "This triangle represents what I refer to as deep desires. Each point represents the deepest desires of my heart. If there are deeper desires, I can't find them. I realize that sounds subjective and a bit unscientific for a doctor, but I think you'll track with me when you consider it."

"Fair enough," Tyler said.

"It was during this season of my life I discovered the first corner of the triangle," pointing to the bottom left corner with his putter. "The other points come later."

Ned etched a "P" at the lower left corner of the triangle.

"I'm in the toughest spot of my life, tougher than my earlier struggles, because now I had a family counting on me. We were all

hurt because of my failure. I was bothered by what others thought
of me, but I was really bothered by how it all affected my family.
What I'd done, the decisions I'd made, and the crash we were experiencing, it took its toll not just on me, but on the people I cared
most about."

Ned laid his putter on the "P."

"This first P, it represents *Protection*."

Tyler nodded.

"I have, and I'd suggest humanity has, a deep desire for our personal well-being. We protect ourselves, as we should. Protection,
I'm convinced, is one of the deep desires that drives us to work.
It's a good desire. If someone drives a golf ball at you, you should
protect yourself. In the morning, you get up and go to work to
provide food and shelter for yourself or for the people you love.
You're driven to protect them. It's good. It's what we should do.
And what bothered me most in that season of life, is not what others thought of me—as painful as that was—but that I'd failed at
this most basic level. I'd made my family vulnerable, and we were
hurting because of it."

"Makes sense."

"Which brings me to Jackson Powell and the conversation I'll
never forget." Ned picked up a rake and smoothed out his whiteboard. "To tell you that story, I've got a question for you. It's a bit
of a trick question, though, so you'll want to consider it carefully."

The two men walked toward their bags and met back at a large
orange cooler placed at the side of the cart path. Tyler, a bit bugged
by his curiosity, but slowly making peace with it, grabbed a cone-
shaped paper cup and filled it with water.

The Fifth Hole

"**W**HAT'S the difference between *hubris* and *despair*?" Ned asked.

"That's the question?"

Ned nodded. The two men tossed their cups in the trash and walked from the orange cooler toward the fifth tee. The fifth hole was a par five with a gentle, almost imperceptible slope from tee to fringe. Three sand traps surrounded the distant green, but other than that, players could relax and just hit the ball.

Tyler considered the question as they both made solid drives. The two men grabbed their bags and Tyler began to process out loud.

"To be honest, I don't use the word *hubris* much, but I think it's a bit like arrogance." Tyler paused as he thought a bit more. "I think of hubris like arrogance on steroids."

Ned looked up toward the distant green. "I like it. Good definition."

"Despair seems opposite to that," Tyler said. "You've lost your confidence. You've run out of options. You don't know where to turn or what to do. If hubris is a bit like arrogance on steroids maybe despair is a bit like insecurity on steroids."

Ned laughed lightly. "I like the way you think. That works for me. *Hubris* is arrogance on steroids. *Despair* is insecurity on steroids. So are they opposites?"

Tyler looked up toward a group of trees, "I'd say so."

"Fair enough. From a certain perspective I agree. Hubris is being full of yourself, it's an extreme form of arrogance. Despair is its opposite. But I wonder if this misses something critical."

Ned lifted his hat a bit and repositioned it on his head.

"I was down, really down, insecurity on steroids you might say. My wife was patient, but she was understandably nervous. She read about a property management job in the paper and threw it in my lap. It was with a company called *The Powell Group*. I'd heard of Jackson Powell but only knew him by reputation. People respected him. He wasn't the wealthiest or most aggressive of investors, but he'd done well, and I knew people looked up to him. I didn't know why, but I was about to find out."

The balls were within fifteen yards of each other. Ned paused as Tyler positioned himself and hit a near perfect shot shy of the green but on track for birdie.

"Nicely done." Ned followed with a well-placed shot fifty yards from the green.

"I made the call and got an interview. I thought the guy was going to tear me up. I'd failed where he'd succeeded. It didn't happen. Jackson Powell was a good man. We talked for a solid hour. He drilled me on my experience and what I'd done and learned. Finally, he shot very straight and denied me the job. He said I could do it, was qualified to do it, but that I shouldn't do it. He said I had more in me than the job demanded, and from his vantage point he knew I'd be in it short-term. He needed a long-term player.

"I understood and welcomed the odd compliment. But then he said something I'll never forget. 'Let me tell you how I see it,' he said. 'You're a talented young man. You're a hardworking young man. You're a smart young man.' Then he paused and looked me straight in the eye, 'But you're a self-centered young man, and your well-being depends on you getting that worked out.'

"I was taken back. I didn't feel self-centered. The self-centered people I knew were full of themselves and arrogant. I welcomed the bold honesty, though. Something within told me to listen carefully to his words. There was something about the man. He was wise. My gut said he was telling me what I needed to hear. I didn't like someone calling me self-centered, but I listened. I must have had a look of confusion on my face. He saw it and addressed it. 'You don't feel self-centered,' he said. 'You feel like a loser.'

"I didn't like the sound of it, but he was right. I nodded, and he went on, 'I've got something you need to hear. I heard it from an old man when I was about your age. He learned it years before from a neighboring farmer when his crops failed. It goes way back. It's called the swing.'"

Ned's steps slowed as he recalled this defining moment in his life, "Mr. Powell stood and walked behind his desk. He pulled a ball of string from a lower drawer and cut a piece about a yard long. He then tied a pen to one end of the string and dropped the pen end to the ground holding the other end in his hand. He then began to swing the pen back and forth, back and forth, like a hypnotist."

Ned pulled out a club, lightly holding it on one end between two fingers, and gently swinging it back and forth.

"While swinging that pen back and forth, he said, 'Ned, this is your life. You're swinging back and forth, back and forth, back and forth.'

"'The left side of the swing we'll call *hubris*. These are the times in life when you're convinced you've got the stuff. You're on top of your game and nothing and nobody can stop you. The right side is where you are now. We'll call it despair. You went from hubris to despair in record time. Circumstances in life changed, and you swung from one side to the other. One day you had it; the next day you didn't.' Then he asked me the exact question I just asked you, 'What's the difference between hubris and despair?'

"I offered a response similar to yours, albeit not as well-worded, but then with that pen swinging back and forth I added, 'One's on the right; the other's on the left.'

"He jumped on that, 'Yes, one's on the right and the other's on the left, but what do they have in common?'

"I thought about it for a moment and stumbled through a few similarities. I mentioned them being the same distance from the center, the same level off the ground, things like that. Then I said, 'They have you in common. Both ends of the swing trace back to your hand.'

"'That's right. They have the same source.'

"The room went silent. The pen kept swinging, and neither of us talked. Mr. Powell finally spoke up, 'What do hubris and despair have in common?'

"I thought about it for what felt like a very long time. I watched that pen go back and forth, I watched his hand. 'Hubris and despair have the same source,' I said, 'You said I'm self-centered. Hubris and despair are two ways of being self-centered.'

"He set the string and pen back on his desk, walked within three feet of where I was sitting, bent over and drilled into me with his eyes, 'Ned, there is no qualitative difference between *hubris* and *despair*,' he said. 'At the surface, they're opposites. Under the surface, at the source, they're identical. Both are self-centered. One is when you're mesmerized with yourself and convinced you've got the goods. With the other, you're still mesmerized with yourself, but you've been knocked to the ground, and you're down for the count. Ned, so long as you stay self-centered, you're going to do nothing but swing back and forth. You'll feel like you change when you swing back and forth. Truth is, you haven't changed; your circumstances changed, as circumstances do. Qualitatively, you're as self-centered as you've ever been, and you're getting taken for a ride.'"

Ned pulled out his pitching wedge and walked to the side of his ball. His shot arched high and landed toward the middle of the green, about ten yards from the pin.

"I was riveted," Ned said as he walked back toward his bag. "I didn't know what to do with what he told me, but I knew I needed to consider it carefully. Jackson Powell had a towering presence. He straightened up, walked behind his large desk and settled into his chair. He then made one of the more obvious but profound observations ever revealed to me. 'Life will always have circumstances swinging back and forth. You will have wins; you will have losses. You will have good days and good years; you will have bad days and bad years. The self-centered swing back and forth with those circumstances. Ned, if you don't figure out how to get yourself off that swing your life will be enslaved to circumstances. You don't want to live the life of a slave. You don't want to be enslaved to me, enslaved to circumstances, enslaved to the whims of some big corporation. You want to be free. You want to go for it in life. You don't want to be controlled by the whims of life's circumstances. Such living is miserable. Ned, you don't just need a job. You'll get one soon enough. You need freedom.'"

Tyler lined up for his shot. The last four years raced through his mind. He could see himself swinging back and forth, from quarter to quarter, as business ebbed and flowed considerably. One quarter, they'd win a couple significant clients, and he'd feel invincible, confident. The next quarter, the economy would hit a speed bump, a client or two would bail or idle back, and he'd kick himself for not better preparing his team for the challenges. A key role of a leader was to foresee the future, and he'd consistently fail at it.

Tyler's shot landed on the upper side of the green and rolled back toward the pin, about four yards from the hole.

"So hubris and despair are different expressions of the same problem—infatuation with ourselves. We look to ourselves, and we either get puffed up or deflated."

"That's been my experience," Ned said. "Hubris and despair are symptoms of the same problem. When a person is arrogant, they can't see past themselves. When a person is insecure, guess what?"

"They can't see past themselves."

"You got it. And the result is a life enslaved to circumstances. We feel good and relatively satisfied when the wind blows in a good direction. But wind is unpredictable. Life is unpredictable. One day your boss thinks highly of you, gives you a raise and a promotion. A quarter or two later and you're packing your personals into a cardboard box and being escorted out of the office."

They walked to their respective shots. Tyler barely noticed when his ball dropped for a birdie. Ned two-putted for par. They picked up their bags and made their way toward the next tee.

"So how do you let life swing around you without being taken for a ride? Is there anything really wrong with being self-centered? I know it sounds bad, but honestly, you've got to take care of yourself. Is it so wrong to care for yourself?"

"That's good. I like that question," Ned said.

"What if what you call being *self-centered* I call being *self-reliant*. One sounds arrogant, but the other sounds responsible. I like people who are self-reliant. It's good to be self-reliant. If that's arrogance, or maybe a cousin of arrogance, then so be it."

"That's excellent. I like the way you think. You're making a critical distinction. I especially like the word *responsible*. I empathize with your value of self-reliance as well. There's nothing more frustrating than working with irresponsible people who are overly reliant on others."

Tyler nodded, recalling a few people he'd had to cut over the years.

"When I'm at a whiteboard facilitating a discussion," Ned said, "we often come into important questions that will send us down a rabbit trail if we address them immediately. We have a practice of carving off a corner of the whiteboard and designating it our 'parking lot.' Your question is excellent, but to address it, we need to give it a bit more context. Let's put it in the parking lot for a few minutes and pull it out a somewhere down toward the next green."

"Fair enough," Tyler said, well-acquainted with the parking lot concept.

As they walked, Tyler couldn't help but notice Ned was tapping on his phone. They were close enough that he could tell he wasn't texting, but far enough that he couldn't see what he was doing. Ned was looking at a website. What would he be looking up in the middle of a game of golf?

The Sixth Hole

"**D**ID I just birdie?" Tyler finally woke up to what he'd just done.

"Well done," Ned smiled and waved Tyler to the tee box.

"I think I will," Tyler said.

"Not bad for a doctor."

The reminder that this conversation was happening under false pretense increasingly bothered Tyler. For the first time in as long as he remembered, he found someone older who at least held potential for an open and honest conversation. Most of the older people he'd experienced in his work life put up false pretense to make themselves look better than they really were. Now here he was, talking with someone who at least seemed genuine, and he wasn't able to be himself. The irony was not lost on him.

"I assume the hole is directly beyond that rise?"

"Yes, a par five."

"And I assume it's a straight shot."

"Yes, a straight shot. The fairway narrows when you get closer to the green. No worries at this point."

Tyler's drive soared down the fairway and bounced three quarters of the way up the rise. Ned followed with a decent drive, resting a few club lengths behind Tyler's.

As they began their walk, Ned went back to his story.

"I left Jackson Powell's office aware of the problem, but I didn't know the solution. I had to get off that swing. I had to get my eyes off me. I had to stop swinging back and forth riding the circumstances of my life. I asked Mr. Powell how to do it. He smiled, told me to give it some thought, and suggested I dig deep into my soul. He told me if I'd give it some thought first he'd be glad to meet with me again to talk it through."

"Not exactly a preacher," Tyler said.

"That's right," Ned said. "He wasn't pushing anything on me. He was just opening the doors. I left his office and went for a long walk around a nearby lake. I walked and walked and walked. I saw that pen swinging back and forth, I saw his hand holding the string, I saw my life going from hubris to despair and back again. I knew the man was right. I had to get off that swing or I'd be miserable. I knew the problem. I was self-centered. I had my eyes on me. So I kept asking and asking, 'How do I get my eyes off me...how do I get my eyes off me?'"

Ned pulled his three wood, carrying it by his side.

"As I walked around that lake I did something I hadn't done in years. I prayed. Actually, it wasn't like a prayer, at least as I had known prayer previously. I just talked with God. That was new for me. It may have been my first real prayer. As I talked, my mind went back to how my so-called relationship with God had ended years before in that church. I started talking to God about my resistance to him and that whole past life of mine. Somewhere in that moment I got to thinking about the Ten Commandments. I thought I was thinking about them because that's how everything blew-up before, and I suppose that's what started my thoughts. But then there was a moment I can only describe as spiritual. It was as if during a pause in my talking to God he whispered something back to me."

Ned rested his bag near his ball.

"It wasn't an audible whisper, but I heard him clearly, '*You shall have no other gods before me.*' It made me smile. That's the first of the Ten Commandments. I didn't so much hear a command—although it most certainly is a command. I heard the whisper of what might become a liberating way of life. By placing my eyes on me, I had placed a god before God...me. I was worshiping me. The thought stopped me in my tracks. I sat down at a bench overlooking the lake. I had no idea what I was going to do to pay the rent, but in that moment I gained a depth of insight I had not known before."

Ned lined up and took his next shot—a low arching shot that bounced and rolled about twenty yards from the green.

"For the first time, I saw what it meant to authentically trust God. I was trusting in my own abilities to make life work. What would it be like if I stopped making myself god, trying to control everything, and started looking to God as if he truly were my God. Life would feel very different if I entrusted my life and problems to God. I instinctively knew this didn't mean I wouldn't work hard and take responsibility for my life. But there was something qualitatively different in the perspective. Moments before, life and well-being rested on my shoulders and was bearing down hard on my back. In that moment, I felt the possibility of the weight of life to be lifted off me, almost physically. What I did next is almost embarrassing."

"More embarrassing than whispers in your head from God?" Tyler barely knew Ned but sensed he could take the mild ribbing.

"Believe it or not, yes, but I couldn't care less. What happened next was a powerful moment in my life. I got up from the bench and started walking. Then I started jogging. Within about thirty seconds, I was in an all-out sprint. I was running as fast as my legs could take me. It must have been a sight to behold, and I don't think I've run like that since, but it was like I'd just been set free, and I couldn't help but express it physically." Ned paused looking off into the distance. "It was the run of a child, innocent and free."

Tyler took his shot as the silence lingered momentarily. His ball landed near Ned's, about fifteen yards from the green.

"Odd maybe, but I get it."

Tyler placed his club in his bag as the two men continued their walk down the fairway. "Now's when we go back to the parking lot. How did you articulate that question?"

"What you called self-centeredness, I called self-reliance or being responsible. What's wrong with being self-reliant, or more plainly, being responsible?"

"Yes, a good observation and important distinction. Let me ask you a question. Let's say you're a financial advisor. And let's say I give you a hundred thousand dollars to invest on my behalf. If you're a responsible advisor, what would you do with that money?"

Tyler considered the question and answered based on his experience. "I'd talk with you about your goals. More than likely I'd put it into an agreed upon mutual fund that best matched your goals and the degree of risk you'd like to take."

"That's good. So the responsible thing to do is to entrust that money to a money manager who knows what he or she is doing."

"That's right."

"But that's not being self-reliant. That's relying on a money manager. How is that not irresponsible?"

Tyler looked toward a small grouping of trees. He looked back. "I get where you're going. I'm responsible by putting your money into the hands of an expert. Most financial advisors aren't the true money gurus. They know the basics but rely on the financial wizards who run the funds to truly determine the best investments."

"That's right," Ned said.

"So my being responsible—as a financial advisor—is to find the best funds run by the best money managers and provide the means for you to entrust your money to them."

"That's correct, so pull that out of the land of metaphors and bring it back to what launched me into my ridiculous run around that lake."

Tyler pulled the towel attached to the top of his bag and wiped sweat from his hands and forearms. "You ran because you found someone who knew more about life than you did, so you effectively entrusted your life to that someone."

"You got it. And this felt anything but irresponsible. If anything, I felt like I was on the brink of finally being responsible. I was taking my hundred thousand dollars—my life—to the money manager who knew a thing or two about life. Instead of looking to myself—what I call being self-centered—I'd look toward God. I never felt so free."

Tyler thought for a moment, recalling a meeting he'd attended with a friend a few years back. Ned pulled his pitching wedge and placed his ball on the near side of the green.

"You know, a few years back I went with a friend to her first AA meeting, Alcoholics Anonymous. It was clear she needed to go but she was understandably scared to do it. I offered to go with her. What you're saying sounds a bit like how they described the first step."

"You're very right," Ned said. "Do you remember how they word it?"

"I do," Tyler said as he lined up for his shot. "The first step is to admit that you're powerless." Tyler's shot bounced over the hole and rolled to a stop ten yards from the pin. "I didn't think much of it at the time. I could certainly tell that my friend was powerless over alcohol. My life was going fairly well at that point, though, so I didn't feel a need to personalize much of it. But as you describe your story, I can see how you're applying a similar concept."

"Very much so," Ned said. "Stepping off that swing has a great deal to do with letting go of our attempt to hold the power and control."

"There's something about it, though," Tyler said. "I get what you're saying. I might even respect it. Something about it grates at me, though. I can't quite articulate it."

"That's good," Ned said. "Listen to that. I suspect it will lead to something important."

The two men closed the hole out in silence, both men shooting par. Tyler wondered what he had gotten himself into, taking a dare worthy of a man ten years younger than himself. He wasn't about to blow it, though.

Not yet, anyway.

The Seventh Hole

THE seventh hole was well known as one of the more challenging holes on the course. It was a par three, simple enough, but the green backed up to a water hazard that hugged the top side of the green a mere six feet from the fringe. Both men pulled their nine irons and readied themselves for short drives.

Tyler watched his ball land beyond the pin and roll to the far side of the green, stopping at the fringe. Ned placed his ball slightly short of the green.

Midway to the green Tyler finally spoke.

"What you say makes sense. And I don't question your personal experience. I don't buy it, though."

"That's good, because I'm not selling anything. Tell me more, though."

Tyler didn't respond immediately, quietly considering how to position his own thoughts through Blake's experience.

"I worked hard to get through med school. I took responsibility for things, I pressed through adversity, and I now have a reliable vocation, even if I don't like where it's landed. People say religion is a crutch for the weak, an over-used cliché probably. But you readily admit you were at a low point. I don't have it all figured out, but I don't want to be someone who has to lean on some God out there for my own well-being. I'd like to think that if there really is a God he'd want me to stand up and be independent."

"That's good. You're processing my experience and holding it up to your own. I like that. Let me ask you a question, though."

Ned paused.

"When you hear my story, does it sound like I'm living life as a needy, overly dependent, weak person?"

Tyler looked toward a pair of ducks sliding to a stop in a nearby water hazard. "I wouldn't word it like that. But you went through hell. You went through bankruptcy. You and your family lost your business, your house, maybe respect of friends. I suspect most anyone going through bankruptcy might call out to some sort of God. Religious stuff seems most applicable for those who need it. You said it yourself, you need God. I don't think I do."

Even as he said this, Tyler wanted to qualify it a bit—he was coming across more together than he intended. He didn't really know who he was speaking for, though. Was he speaking as himself or as Blake? Whoever he was, he decided to let his comments stand.

"It's a fair comment. I would have said it myself earlier in life. I wouldn't have had the guts to say it before I walked away from church years ago, but I said similar things between then and the day I met with Jackson Powell. But your comments make an assumption. Actually they make a few assumptions."

As he walked, Ned pulled his pitching wedge. "I want you to do something. It's a little odd, but hear me out on this."

Tyler increasingly didn't know what to expect from Ned Peterson.

"We're twenty yards from the green. Hold your breath until you get to your ball."

"Hold my breath?"

Ned nodded.

"Why?"

"Just hold your breath."

Tyler felt a bit foolish, but who really cared? He'd hold his breath.

As Tyler neared the green Ned commented, "How are you doing Doctor? You want some air yet? How's it feel?"

As he neared his ball Tyler finally let go and took a breath.

"You're breathing a little hard. Why?"

Tyler didn't answer.

"There must be something wrong with you. You need air. Air is only for the weak. It's a crutch."

Tyler looked at Ned, "And your point is?"

Ned lined up for a chip shot that landed five yards from the hole and rolled another two. Tyler's putt ringed the hole and rolled two feet away.

Sure, he needed air, Tyler thought to himself, but that certainly didn't mean he needed God.

"Go ahead and close out the hole."

Tyler tapped his ball in as Ned lined up for what ended up being a putt for par.

"You're saying I have needs," Tyler finally spoke.

"Yes. Many of them."

"And you're saying needs don't necessarily indicate a flaw."

Ned nodded.

Tyler placed the pin in the hole and handed Ned his ball. They walked separately to their bags, and came back together at a path leading under a bridge to the next hole.

"But things like food and air, these are just basic human needs. It's like a car that needs gas."

Ned said nothing.

"And you would say a basic need of humanity is a need for God—not a flaw or weakness just who we are."

"You got it. When I walked round that lake years ago I realized I was a very religious man. I had a god. I was devout. My god was me. As I've grown in my understanding, I'm increasingly convinced my experience is not unique. We all base our lives upon something. There's something upon which we stand. This is true no matter how our lives are going, whether we're in bankruptcy or flying high. We are designed, I'm convinced, to trust in something. Being self-centered, riding the swing between hubris and despair, was my attempt at being my own god. I discovered I needed to fire my god. My god was inadequate for the job. I wasn't qualified. I needed God to be my God. He had a much better resume."

They were now at the tee box for the eighth hole.

"Your comment, though—that it's all about a crutch—makes a couple of other assumptions. That's just the first."

"And the second?" Tyler wasn't sure if he was interested or not, but he was already in the deep end of the swimming pool.

"You're assuming you're not broken."

"Not broken?"

"That's right. When you say you don't need a crutch, you're assuming you're not broken. I'd challenge that assumption. It wouldn't matter if you weren't broken. You'd still need God. I'm convinced we're all designed to need God—just like we need air or food or friendship—and that's a good thing, but the need is only heightened by the painful reality of our brokenness."

Tyler's eyes squinted slightly as he turned the thought in his mind.

Ned smiled, "If you try to convince me you're not broken, a few simple questions would surface plenty of angles to consider it from."

Tyler had no objections to his well-known brokenness. He welcomed the nudge. He knew he was putting up somewhat of a front but found it challenging to be himself when he wasn't being himself. A surprising thought came to mind. He wished he could be open with this man. The charade would keep that from happening.

"I'd welcome the questions, but no need. My brokenness is clear enough."

The two men readied for the next drive as Tyler wondered how Blake would have engaged this conversation. Despite his growing frustration with not being able to be himself, Tyler looked forward to Lola's and debriefing the day. He'd nearly made it through the first nine holes without blowing his cover.

Once again, Ned looked at his phone. Tyler could see he was on the Internet but couldn't see what he was doing. Why would Ned be on the Internet now?

The Eighth Hole

THE eighth hole was a shorter par four, but it had a strong dogleg to the left midway down the fairway that made placement important. Ned's shot landed where the fairway turned, well-placed for his second shot. Tyler nailed it, his ball hugging the trees and turning gently with the fairway but still in sight.

"Any more assumptions?"

"Actually, yes," Ned said.

They picked up their bags and began the walk down the fairway.

"You know any of the classic stories from the Bible?"

"I might be familiar with a couple if you mentioned them, but I doubt it."

"How about David and Goliath?"

"I know the basics of the story. I don't know the details, though."

"David's young," Ned said. "He's not old enough to go out to battle for real. He made it to the front lines because his dad sent him to check on his older brothers. While there, he hears Goliath taunting the Israelite warriors. Goliath's enormous. None of the Israelite warriors are willing to step up to this man. If you think of Jackson Powell's illustration, these warriors were on the despair side of the swing. They saw a large and experienced warrior who could take any one of them with ease. They were comparing his strength and ability to their own strength and ability, and they saw they didn't have the goods. They were self-centered, and when they looked at themselves they saw inadequacy."

"Sounds reasonable," Tyler said.

"Yes, it does, but not to young David. David had a different perspective on the situation. He took offense at Goliath's taunts. To David, Goliath wasn't speaking against the Israelite army; he was speaking against the Israelite's God. David's words to Goliath were stunning. I know them well, because there's been more than one occasion in my life when they went ringing through my ears to give me the courage I needed. Young David, with no armor, steps out onto the battlefield. He must have looked pathetic, but he cries out, '*You come against me with sword and spear and javelin; I come against you in the name of the Lord Almighty, the God of the armies of Israel, whom you have defied.*'

"So this teenage boy is trash talking a seasoned warrior. He stares him down and lets him know the source of his seemingly insane confidence. 'My power's not in these rocks or this sling, my power's in the fact that God's got my back.'"

"So David, you're saying, wasn't on the swing, he'd found a way off."

"That's right," Ned said. "His eyes weren't on himself. His eyes were on God. With his eyes on God—rather than on the circumstances swinging around him—he had courage. This courage was foreign to the other warriors."

"So what's that have to do with an assumption?"

Ned rested his bag and pulled his three iron. His shot landed to the left of the green on a ridge beside a sand trap.

"You said religion is a crutch—something for the weak. The implication is that it's for those who can't cut it on their own, the soft among us."

"Something like that."

Ned said nothing else, seemingly content to let Tyler connect the dots.

"Faith didn't make David a wimp. It made him a warrior." Tyler finally said.

"Well said. By saying faith is for the weak, you're implying that people of faith lead soft lives. And to be sure, I get it. People of false faith do—very often—lead soft lives. I can't see into another person's heart any more than the next guy, but it doesn't take much to smell professing faith that isn't real faith. I call this plastic faith. Plastic faith doesn't get people off the swing. They know the doctrines, but their lives radiate the insecurity and arrogance associated with swinging back and forth. So I get why a person like yourself might think matters of faith are for wimps. Authentic faith, though, inspires people toward a kind of liberated and courageous living I could only dream about when I was living a self-centered life.

Tyler pulled his seven iron and lined up for his shot. It landed in the sand trap just behind Ned's ball.

"So are you suggesting only people with your faith do courageous things?"

"Not at all. Not even close. People do courageous things all the time. I would say, though, that all acts of courage are rooted in faith in something. Think about David compared to the real warriors. Those were the guys who should have taken on Goliath. It was their job to do so. Their faith was placed in themselves, though, which resulted in fear-based living. They looked at Goliath and said, 'Not me!' David's faith in God compelled him to advance, because his God was bigger than Goliath. On the outside David didn't look tough at all. He looked pathetic. But on the inside he was tough as nails. The world needs more men and women of genuine faith. These are the people who step across the line and square off with life's Goliaths. Take a pass through the Scriptures, and you discover men and women of valor. They engaged life. They stood up against extreme odds and conquered. These were no softies."

"What Goliaths have you downed?" Tyler's question was sincere.

Ned paused for a moment, "That question is bigger than you realize."

"How so?"

Ned repositioned his bag on his shoulder.

"After my all-out run around the lake I sat at a bench and looked out over the water. I knew the problem, life would have its swings. There would be ups and downs. I needed to get my eyes off me. I needed God. I could see my car in the distance. I looked at my car and was reminded that life would not be lived running around the lake, no matter how free I felt. Life would be lived when I got back in that car and engaged the problems I was facing, and my problems were enormous. I had financial problems, marriage problems, vocational problems, and a few problems I haven't told you about, but would be glad to if we have time. My life was very broken. In a matter of minutes, whether I liked it or not, I would be eyeball to eyeball not just with Goliath, but with what felt like an army of Goliaths. Ultimately, though, I made a decision that transformed the way I approach life."

"And what was that?" Tyler asked while stepping into the sand trap near his ball. The pin was at least fifteen yards away. He mastered this shot years ago, but was still a bit rusty on it since his return to golf. He got out of the trap, but barely onto the green.

"Put plainly, I decided to not live for survival. The initial battles were digging my way out of a hole. Call them 'defense' if you will. These are the Goliaths you're referring to when you say you understand that some people need God. But there are other Goliaths I'd call 'offense.'" Ned walked to the edge of the sand trap and picked up a rake. With it, he again etched a triangle. He wrote a P at the bottom left corner of the first triangle, representing *protection*, and then wrote a second P, this one at the top of the first triangle.

"I say your question is a bigger question than you realize, because it takes you to the apex of the triangle."

"Does the apex have significance?"

"You could say that. It's certainly at the top for a reason. The top is dependent upon how we address the bottom two corners, and it has to do with why we're here, why we're alive." Ned paused as he leaned on the rake. "Any guesses as to what the apex might represent."

Tyler considered Ned's comments. "Based on what you just said, about it having to do with why we're here, I'd guess *purpose*."

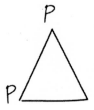

"You got it. I have, and I'm convinced humanity has, a deep desire to lead a life that matters. And I say that in reference to your question about life's Goliaths, because after my failures, it was incredibly tempting to make my life simply about survival." Ned moved the rake to the lower left *protection* corner. "More than anything, I just wanted to get my head above water."

Tyler nodded.

"But it was fascinating what happened when I began to authentically engage God. God wasn't interested in my life merely being about survival." Ned moved the rake back to the apex of the triangle. "He consistently nudged me. I didn't want to be nudged, but he didn't let me get into a victim's mentality or survival mode. He kept telling me my protection was taken care of. He wanted me to trust him with me and my family. The more I was able to do that, the more liberated I became."

"How so?"

"The less I had to obsess over my well-being, my protection, the more I was liberated to consider others. I can't tell you how counter-intuitive this was for a guy who had been through what I'd been through. But it has proved to be a liberated life. It's freedom. I don't have to obsess over my own protection. I entrust it to God. He of course leads and guides me toward responsible actions, but there's a qualitative difference in how I live when my protection rests in his hands rather than my own self-protective ways. I'm no longer that Israelite warrior afraid of Goliath. I'm increasingly—albeit imperfectly—like David, able and willing to move forward rather than cower back. The more I do this, the more purpose I come into," Ned bounced the rake on the apex of the triangle.

Ned's chip shot rolled toward the pin, stopping club-length from the hole.

Tyler considered Ned's description. "So by addressing your deep desire for protection, you're free to address your deep desire for meaning and purpose."

"That's it. Life isn't just about survival. We know that instinctively."

Tyler finished raking the sand trap, placed his sand wedge in his bag and pulled his putter.

"What kind of 'offense' have you engaged?"

Ned placed a ball marker by his ball and picked up the ball, clearing the way for Tyler's long putt. "In recent years, my wife and I, along with our church, have invested heavily in a project that works with partners in third world countries to free young women from sex trafficking. When my wife was a college student, many years ago, she visited Thailand. When there, her heart broke by what she saw with young girls deceptively brought into what we now call sex trafficking."

Tyler's putt passed the hole by about a yard.

"Early in our relationship, she told me how she wanted to do something about it. I resonated with the cause but it felt so foreign and distant to me, I quietly doubted we'd ever really be able to do anything about it."

Ned placed his ball by his marker and lined up for his putt.

"When our faith started to take flight, though, her passion for this cause came alive again."

Ned's putt sank in the hole.

"Instead of dismissing it as a good cause we could never do anything about, I decided to talk with God about it and see if we might discover ways we could make a difference. Since then, on our own and with our church, we've been part of starting and supporting safe houses for women in three different countries, one of which is right here in the U.S. We're in way over our heads. It involves most every discipline you can muster: law, counseling, finances. It's psychological, it's spiritual, it's highly relational."

Ned went quiet as Tyler lined up and sank his putt.

"Our little church has literally made a difference in the lives of these young gals on continents far from here. I never thought it would have been possible."

Tyler had read a bit about the issue. "I bet that's rewarding," he said. "I don't want to sound like I'm questioning the validity of your work. I admire what you're doing. But in the context of this conversation, I can't help but think of people doing that very same work without a faith in God."

"Absolutely true, and I admire their work. But again, I'd suggest they're trusting in *something*. Whatever that *something* is, is effectively their god. What I discovered was that when I switched and let God be my God, I tapped into a power and a presence that empowered bold action that transcends what I bring when left to myself."

Ned handed the pin to Tyler as Tyler handed Ned his ball.

"And let me give you full disclosure, because I'm not trying to prove something or make something look better than it is. This whole adventure, going all the way back to that walk around the lake, it hasn't come easy. The Goliaths of this life taunt us. I'd be dishonest if I didn't admit there are times those taunts get to me. It's going to sound odd, but there was a moment back at that lake I still think about from time to time. I was about to walk back to my car, and I picked up a small rock. With the rock in my hand, I said a short prayer, 'God, I've made a mess of my life. It's been a hard ride swinging back and forth with life's circumstances. From this day forward my eyes are off me and on you. I put the old me on this rock, and I bury it in this lake.' I threw that rock as far into the lake as I could. I watched it splash and sink out of sight. It was my way of trash talking Goliath. When I feel the Goliaths of life taunting me, whether it be something that threatens my protection or a challenge I'm facing living out my purpose, I think about that rock sinking out of sight."

Tyler smiled. He liked Ned Peterson.

"When I got home my wife could see it in my eyes. I was more alive at that moment than I had ever been in all my days. The best description is simply the word freedom. I was free from the swing. I was toe to toe with Goliath and was encouraged in the truest sense of the word—courage had been put in me."

"What'd you tell your wife?"

"I started by telling her what I've told you. I told her about Jackson Powell, his honesty, and the swing. I told her about my thoughts at the lake. I told her about the rock, the stand I'd taken, and then I did something I didn't expect, but definitely needed to do."

"What's that?"

"I apologized."

Tyler nodded.

"I'd been a very difficult man to live with. And this wasn't just about my financial struggles. I was difficult when times were good. On either side of the swing I was trouble. When times were good, I obsessed about my work because it seemed so fragile. When times were rough, I obsessed about my work because I was frightened. Anxiety and fear are contagious, and they have implications for the way you treat the people around you. I'd never shown real emotion, but on that day, through tears I told her how sorry I was. She knew I was sincere."

Both men walked toward the ninth hole.

Tyler was silent. His mind again went to Blake. More than anyone he knew, Blake wanted a life that mattered. It's why he'd become a doctor and why he was frustrated with his current situation. Yes, he made a difference, but not like he thought he could in a third world setting, far away from the cluttered challenges of healthcare. Tyler wondered how this conversation might affect Blake. He didn't regret taking the dare. He did wonder, though, how Blake might get time with this guy.

Tyler's answer would come sooner than he expected.

The Ninth Hole

THE ninth hole was played in silence. Tyler was feeling as much as he was thinking. Memories, recent and long past, washed over him as he played a near perfect hole. He wasn't sad, mad, or frustrated, just sober and a bit contemplative.

As he crossed the green to pick up the pin, Tyler wished he could give Ned the real Tyler O'Brien story. Ned Peterson had a depth and an authenticity he'd rarely, if ever, encountered. He would welcome an opportunity to talk through recent events. Knowing it couldn't be, he posed a question while walking toward the hole with the pin.

"Ned, a hole or two back, you commented on brokenness. You said if I didn't see my own brokenness that a few simple questions would surface plenty of it if I'd be willing to be open." Tyler knew he was taking a risk but decided to go for it. "What questions did you have in mind?"

Tyler hoped this question would allow them to talk about his life without talking about his life.

A slight grin appeared on Ned's face as he dropped his putter into his bag. "Well, you really want me to ask?"

Tyler thought for a moment, "Yeah, I do."

Ned nodded, "Alright then, my first question's fairly obvious."

"Alright, what is it?"

Ned's response was succinct. "What's your real name?"

Tyler's head jerked toward Ned. "My real name?"

"Yes, what's your real name. I've never met Blake Hill, but you're definitely not him."

"Definitely?"

"Definitely."

A smile crossed Tyler's face. "And, why would you think I'm not him?"

Ned returned the smile as he picked up his bag. "I was fairly certain no less than thirty minutes after we meet. It took a bit longer to confirm it, but there's no doubt."

"Fair enough. Make your case."

"My case?" Ned smiled. "Well, for starters, I knew Blake didn't want to meet with me. It didn't cross my mind that he'd send a representative in his name, but that's the context."

Tyler nodded as Ned continued.

"Then, on the second hole, I asked what kind of medicine you practice. You said internal medicine. No big deal, but the way you explained it made no sense at all."

Tyler looked at Ned, realizing he wasn't going to recover from this.

"You brushed off the conversation by saying you were sick of your work, that you'd been in surgery, or something like that. But as the name implies, doctors specializing in internal medicine don't do surgery. They treat internal organs through non-surgical means, like medicine. At first I gave you the benefit of the doubt thinking medical advancement could have blurred the lines, as I suspect it has in some cases."

"Anything else?"

"Yes. It seemed odd that a guy driving that piece of junk you hit with a golf ball would be able to cover for a doctor's losses in Vegas. No big deal, but it influenced my thoughts. Curiosity got the best of me. A few holes back, I used my phone and Googled 'Dr. Blake Hill.' A few photos came up. They're definitely not you."

Tyler smiled—clearly caught—and asked, "Why'd you let the conversation go?"

Ned shrugged. "I found the whole thing entertaining."

Tyler laughed, relieved but not entirely surprised by Ned's good nature.

"Why ruin a good moment?" Ned said, "How you got into this will be interesting to hear, but I was enjoying knowing it was happening."

Tyler extended his hand. "I'm Tyler O'Brien. Good to meet you. I hope you're not offended. I can explain, but let's just say there's a girl involved."

"Enough said. And I'd guess it's safe to assume you're not a doctor."

"Very safe."

"And your gambling habits?"

"Blake's doing fine."

Ned laughed. "I love it."

They walked in silence with the obvious question of Tyler's real vocation hanging in the air. The ninth hole ended near the clubhouse. A meandering pathway took them toward the tenth tee.

"So tell me about the real Tyler. What do you do?"

"Not much, right now," Tyler said. "It's been an interesting week."

"Interesting?"

"Yes, to say the least. Last week was eventful."

"Sounds like the not-so-good kind of eventful."

Tyler wiped his nine iron with a towel as they walked. "I have no regrets. I did the right thing. I'm not sure what you'll think of the way I did it, though."

"Try me."

Tyler looked toward Ned. "You won't believe it if I tell you." He shook his head but then added, "Actually, maybe you would. Your snapping story sounded dangerously familiar."

Ned smiled. "Something tells me this is going to be good."

"Depends how you define good." Tyler laughed.

And with that, Tyler O'Brien was finally ready to tell his real story.

THE
BACK
NINE

The Tenth Hole

NED stood after placing his ball on the tee. "So you're not a doctor, and last week was eventful."

"Yes, until last week I was president of a small software company."

Ned took a patient but firm swing, his shot landing a bit off center but respectably down the fairway. "What happened last week?"

Tyler pulled his driver, grabbed a fresh tee, and stepped into the tee box.

"Last week needs a little context." Tyler leaned over to place his ball on the tee. "You know what a mantra is?" Tyler asked as he rose.

"In the business sense, I suspect you mean a company's mission statement or something like that."

"Actually, not typically, but you might think that. Mission statements are known; mantras are felt. Our company has a mission statement. It's on the first page of the employee handbook and doesn't get much airtime past new employee orientation."

"You mean it's not on t-shirts for the company picnic?"

Tyler gently swung his driver back and forth.

"It's made it on a t-shirt or two, maybe a coffee mug, but our mission statement doesn't impact our daily work. Our mantra, on the other hand, will never be on a t-shirt, never be on our website, and never be emblazoned on the lobby wall."

"But you live it."

Tyler stopped swinging his club and looked toward Ned. "We. Make. Plan. That's our mantra."

Ned gently laughed and nodded as Tyler lined up and hit a long ball down the center of the fairway. Tyler placed his driver in his bag and the two men began to walk.

"Those three words define my life—or at least they did until last week. Everything stands or falls on making plan, hitting the numbers. My company is owned by a larger company that incubates start-ups and takes them public. Consistently making plan is essential for an IPO."

"You need to show you're not only profitable but you know your business."

"That's right. Miss the mark by a few points and Wall Street will punish you severely. We're not yet public, but from day one we acted as if we were. This isn't just for training purposes. It's so we can show future investors not just our vision for the future but our solid performance in the past."

"Makes sense."

"It does, but it breaks down when you have leaders at the helm who are out of touch with reality."

"Weren't you the leader?"

"I was, but I reported to the board of directors, and most specifically, the chairman of the board, a guy named Tom Phelps."

"Good guy?"

Tyler looked down the fairway and then back at Ned.

"You ever run on treadmills?"

"As little as possible. I prefer walking out here."

"Imagine this. You're at the gym. You step on a treadmill. You hit the start button, and it begins to roll. You're at a comfortable speed, but you want a solid work-out. You hit the speed button and increase the rotation. You do this two or three times until you find a speed that works. It's doable, but it's a stretch."

"I'm with you."

"Now I walk up. I say hello. You nod. I then reach over and press your speed button a few times. You give me an odd look, but you pick up your pace. I look at you and see you're doing alright, a bit more sweat, but you're making it. I do it again. You give me another odd look. Your jog begins to feel like a run. Finally, I reach over and really crank it up. Now your run's a sprint. A look of fear crosses your face. You're running so hard you can't get your hand to the speed button. You feel like your heart's going to burst. Your lungs are burning. And then I do it again. I crank up the speed with three more pushes of the button. It's too much. You collapse. You get burn marks on your skin from the spin of the treadmill. I'm nowhere to be seen."

They slowed their walk as they neared Ned's ball. "So you're the guy on the treadmill, and Tom's the guy reaching over and recklessly increasing the speed."

"Exactly."

Ned rested his bag and pulled his three wood.

"Tom Phelps is a pompous son of a very rich man. His money came from his dad, the elderly Tom Phelps, Sr., who is a good man. Tom Phelps, Jr. is highly intelligent but lacks street wisdom. He has zero sense of what really goes on day to day. He barely works. He'll roll in toward the end of each month, look at the numbers, and ask nothing of the real business."

"Sounds like the classic, 'Dad makes a pile of money and doesn't spend it. Son takes the reins and acts like he's a business genius who's earned it all'—an old money scenario."

Ned lined up for his shot. His ball arched high and bounced about ten yards to the left of the green.

"It doesn't always work that way, but it certainly has in this case. I know my business. Each year my team and I created a plan that would stretch us. It was based on our understanding of the business. We didn't make these numbers up. The plan we created was designed to take us to the next level in a way that demanded that we worked hard and performed. Every single one of us wanted to win. We wanted that solid track record as much as any of the investors wanted it."

"And Tom reaches in," Ned said, "cranks up the speed, and wonders why you and the others wind up on the floor with treadmill burns."

"That's an understatement. We set goals that stretch us just beyond what any of us think we could do. But the goals are rooted in an understanding of the business and an understanding that if we work hard and perform, we can do it. Tom's goals are rooted in unbridled greed that ruins our lives. Last year, we created a plan. The entire leadership team gulped when we signed on to it. We knew we were going to have to work both hard and smart to hit those numbers. Tom marched into a single meeting and insisted we increase the plan by twenty-three percent. It was ridiculous."

Tyler paused.

"I've got money, Ned, but I don't have a life."

Ned nodded as Tyler pulled his three iron and lined up for his shot.

"There's this gal I met about six months ago while running. She was running with her dog and had stopped at a drinking fountain to give him water. I'd stopped as well, and we got talking. There wasn't much to it, but after that, I kept running into her. I saw her when running again the next Saturday, and a few days later at a coffee shop. We both thought it was pretty odd, so I asked for her number. She gave it to me. It felt like I was supposed to get to know her."

Tyler's shot landed just beyond the green, a short pitch from the rough.

"What happened?"

"I got caught up in work. Like I said, it's been six months." Tyler pulled out his wallet, as the two men walked, and dug out a little slip of paper. "Here's the number. Not only have I not called, but I haven't even run since then."

"Sounds like the treadmill is burning through your skin."

"To say the least. My health, my friendships, zeal for life, all of it's tanked."

The silence lingered and Ned finally spoke up, "So what happened last week?"

A grin crossed Tyler's face, "Last week was the annual banquet."

Ned turned toward Tyler, "The annual banquet, huh? Am I to assume this is where the snapping comes into play."

"Trouble is brewing," Tyler said with a smile. "The annual banquet is the executive teams from seven sister companies. These are companies owned or heavily invested in by Tom Phelps, Sr., the father of my beloved chairman. It's a sizable group. Every executive in that room makes good money, but the biggest money comes in the form of year-end bonuses. It comes down to one thing and one thing only."

"We make plan," Ned said.

"You got it. When you make plan you win big. Bonus checks are cut that afternoon. The banquet, though, is less about the cash and more about celebrating the win. It's all about getting a little 'w' by your name."

"Is it safe to assume you didn't make plan?"

"Actually, no. We made plan, but I wouldn't say we made plan with our integrity intact. My team performed flawlessly, but by the end of the third quarter it was clear we weren't on trajectory. There's more than one way to make plan, though, and Tom Phelps isn't shy about creative accounting to make it happen. It wasn't blatantly illegal, but we certainly pushed the limits of acceptable accounting practices."

Ned nodded with understanding.

"We made plan for the fourth year in a row, which is the amount of time I've been there. I was given rock star treatment. They asked me to make a speech."

"A speech?"

"Yes, a speech."

"A speech sounds like a prime opportunity for trouble."

Tyler nodded.

Ned pulled his pitching wedge and placed his bag beside the green. A knowing look crossed his face.

"You didn't," Ned said.

"I most certainly did."

The story paused as the two men were forced to walk to separate sides of the green.

Tyler pulled the pin. The story hung between them, but neither man spoke as they closed out the hole.

"So what happened?" Ned asked as his replaced the pin.

Tyler noted a look of genuine anticipation on Ned's face.

This was going to be fun...sort of.

The Eleventh Hole

As they walked toward the eleventh tee, Tyler set the stage for the drama.

"The banquet is always held at the top floor of the Empress Club downtown. The place is impressive. Have you been there?"

"Couple times. Great view."

"Yes, it's quite the place. I arrived a bit late. Everyone was standing around dressed to impress with wine glasses in one hand and napkins with food I can't pronounce in the other. I was late for a reason, though. I didn't want to go. I didn't want to talk. I didn't want to eat. I definitely didn't want to give a speech as if I'd done something heroic. I'd done nothing heroic by making plan."

Ned nodded as they rested their bags at a bench by the tee box.

"Once there I quickly downed a couple glasses of wine and struck up a conversation with a man named Jim Cooper. Jim's a tremendous guy. He grew up in the inner city and was raised by his grandmother, whom I've met. She raised him well and raised him tough. He's African American, and she refused to let him be intimidated by racial barriers. He's smart and hardworking, but I'd heard his year didn't exactly go well."

"Didn't make plan?" Ned pulled his driver and stepped into the tee box.

"That's right, but there's more to it than that. About six years ago, Jim and his wife, Anita, lost a child to leukemia. I didn't know them at the time, and haven't talked much to them about it, but I do know they donate their yearly bonus to a foundation that funds research for more effective ways to treat leukemia." Tyler shook his head. "These are good people who have experienced tragic loss."

Tyler paused as Ned lined up for his drive, a high-arching shot that had distance but landed just within the rough on the right side of the fairway.

"I think very highly of them," Tyler said as he stepped into the tee box. "When I saw Jim I pulled him aside and got the real story about him not making plan. He was reluctant to share, but I got it out of him. He missed plan for good reason. He'd initially set their targets based on his and his team's knowledge of the business, but Tom—true to form—injected the plan with steroids and increased the numbers by thirty percent. Jim objected to no avail, and his team worked hard to hit the inflated number. With two months to go in the year, they were on trajectory to be about twenty-five percent short."

"So they were around his initial projections."

"That's right, but it gets worse."

Tyler lined up for his shot. His ball bounced near Ned's and rolled toward the left side of the fairway.

"So Tom, of course, came in and put pressure on Jim to engage in a little creative accounting, just like he did with me but worse. I won't belabor the details, but this was beyond putting your best foot forward, and even beyond what he'd done with my company. Jim would have none of it. He refused and Tom eventually backed off, but not without letting Jim know he was on the bubble."

Tyler wiped his hand on a towel.

"So to put it bluntly," Tyler said, "Jim stood his ground where I hadn't."

"I get it," Ned said.

Tyler continued talking as they walked toward Ned's ball.

"So there I am, on the brink of being honored, and the person who did the honorable thing, at the expense of a cause he cared deeply about, is not only not getting a check, but is currently at risk of losing his job. This sent me right up to the edge. What happened next pushed me over."

Tyler turned toward Ned.

"Everyone finally made their way to their seats. I grabbed a third glass of wine. Janis Cunningham, one of the board members and a former CEO, welcomed everyone and the food started to roll. After Janis, Tom got up and began what appeared to be a speech. He spoke very highly of me. He told of my great success, but he did more than that. He positioned me against 'other leaders' who 'didn't have the courage to do what it takes to make plan.' I was stunned. Not only was he making me out to be a hero I'm not, but he was taking a veiled—but very clear—shot at Jim." Tyler paused and shook his head. "To an outsider, it would appear

I should have been grateful—not even close. I was furious."

Ned rested his bag and pulled out his three iron. Tyler waited as Ned's shot, a long line drive, bounced and rolled to a stop about fifteen yards shy of the green. Ned grabbed his bag, and they walked toward Tyler's ball.

"I looked across the room at Jim. I already respected the man, but my respect went up from the brief conversation I had with him before we sat down. And as I looked at him I was struck by what I saw."

Tyler stood next to his ball but didn't yet line up for his shot. He leaned his club against his side and looked toward Ned.

"Jim's wife leaned toward him as they sat side by side. She had her hand in his. They looked bold and confident. I was sitting there thinking, 'Look at what they have. They won't get a big check, but their life is rich. Me? I'll get a bump to my bottom line, but the closest thing I have to what they have is a wrinkled piece of paper with a phone number for a gal I met but never called.'"

Tyler lined up and took his shot. His ball bounced off the green and just past the fringe on the right side near a sand trap.

"And then it happened," Tyler said as he placed his four iron back into his bag.

"What happened?"

"I snapped."

Ned smiled.

"Tom just couldn't stop."

The two men walked down the fairway.

"Give that man a microphone and a spotlight, and he can dribble on for hours. I couldn't take it anymore, so I got up from my seat and walked over to a waiter. Tom looked at me oddly, as did a few others, but it wasn't yet too out of the ordinary. I asked the waiter for a pen, and he disappeared for a minute, came back, and handed me a pen. I walked over to Anita Cooper, Jim's wife, bent down behind her and asked for the name of the cancer foundation they support. She told it to me, and I pulled out my bonus check, which I had in my coat pocket. I then signed the check over to the cancer foundation and walked to the side of the podium. Tom looked at me, and I said, 'Are you done yet?'"

Ned smiled and shook his head.

"This caught Tom off guard and made for a wide-eyed crowd. He didn't know what to say, so I kept going, 'I don't know if you're done yet, but I am. I'm done chasing your unbridled greed.' I then turned to the crowd. 'Friends, Tom here is full of B.S. and we all know it. I've done nothing heroic, neither has he, and I'm certainly no success worthy of being honored.' I then raised my check in the air. 'Here's my bonus check. I've just signed it over to a cancer foundation dedicated to researching more effective ways of treating childhood leukemia.' Everyone in the room knew I was standing behind Jim with that. 'Consider this my final act as an employee of this ridiculous regime.' And with that, I walked out of the room, handing the check to a stunned but smiling Anita Cooper along the way."

Ned laughed and shook his head, "How'd everybody react?"

Tyler pulled his pitching wedge and swung it by his side.

"It was simultaneously awkward and electric. The room went quiet, but eyes were wide with excitement, and I saw more than a few heads nodding. My phone lit up with texts of affirmation over the next hour, so generally speaking, people got it. Best of all, I got a call from Anita Cooper the next day and then again a few days later. My gift inspired others to give as well. They'd already received a hundred and twenty-two thousand dollars toward the cause in addition to what I'd given."

Ned stood by his ball. A grin crossed his face. He leaned his pitching wedge against his side, looked up at Tyler, and gave him a one-man standing ovation, "Tyler O'Brien, you're my hero."

Ned's pitch rolled a short putt from the hole. "Any regrets the next day?"

"None. That moment was a two for one."

"Two for one?"

"Yes, I simultaneously stuck it to the man while advancing an important cause."

Ned laughed.

Tyler reassessed his response as he rested his bag and stepped toward his ball. "Actually, let me make a distinction. No, I don't regret my actions at the banquet. I know I burned a bridge, but I also shocked the system, and that might prove helpful to what I do regret. I regret not taking my stand far sooner in a way that would have been more productive and helpful to the company I ran."

Tyler's shot landed club-length from the hole.

"I didn't make a mistake in leaving, but there is much about the past few years I don't feel good about."

Tyler walked toward his ball as Ned pulled the pin. "I'd feel good about it had I taken my stand before compromising my integrity and creating an unhealthy company culture. I'm glad to be out of there, but I don't know what I'll do moving forward. I already got a call from a former colleague who wants me to come be their VP of Sales. I've yet to return the call. I need some space."

"I can see that," Ned said.

The two men closed out the hole. Ned wore a slight smile, periodically shaking his head and laughing to himself. As they walked toward their bags, Tyler posed a question.

"Ned, clearly you're respectful. You don't jam your opinions down my throat, but I really want to know what you think. Give me your no-holds-barred opinion. Do you think I've screwed my life?"

Ned walked without responding. "It depends," he finally said.

"It depends?"

"Yes. The value of last week's move is hanging in the balance. It depends on what you do next, and I'm not referring to you finding another job. You'll do that in due course. But you don't just need a new job. If all you get is a new job you'll fall into the same ruts and routines that led to snapping last week. If that happens, then last week is a waste, because the next job won't be the answer. It will just be another verse in the same old song."

Tyler could hear the wisdom in Ned's assessment.

Ned gently continued, "You need to drop a new ball; that's clear enough. But before you hit that ball you need to give thought to what caused the first ball to land in the wrong fairway. Miss that and at best you'll rip a long shot into the rough."

The two men remained silent. He had yet to articulate it, but Tyler instinctively knew he couldn't keep hitting the ball with the same warped form. There was a time in his life when he thought the answer was to accumulate a pile of money so he wouldn't have to work anymore. He'd done that, though, and ultimately got bored and landed in the job he'd just left. Maybe he'd do something with seemingly more intrinsic value.

"Maybe I should drop this career in corporate leadership altogether. The apex of your triangle comes to mind. I need a stronger sense of purpose. Maybe I should be a teacher or an inner-city mentor."

Ned reflected on the comment before responding. "Do you think that would help?" he finally asked.

"I honestly don't know," Tyler said.

Ned looked toward Tyler as they walked toward the twelfth tee. "Let me ask you a bold question," he finally said. "And let me preface the question by saying, I've done what you've done. There have been plenty of times in my life when I didn't stand my ground, and I should have. So my question has zero judgment in it and a great deal of understanding. What I've found helpful, though, is the 'Why?' question. Why didn't I stand my ground? What was going on inside me? Why did I do what I did? I'm suggesting you consider your form before dropping another ball. To best do that, you need clarity on what really happened."

They paused next to a ball-washer as Tyler considered the question. "To be fair to myself, there are aspects of this past experience that were outside my control. That's not an excuse. It's just reality."

"I don't doubt that," Ned said.

"Despite the fact that I disliked the chairman, I wanted to perform well in his eyes. And there are others who run in the same circles, I wanted to perform well for them."

"Why?"

Tyler picked up his bag. The two men walked slowly toward the twelfth tee.

"These are people I respect. I wanted them to respect me. They're high performers, and they respect high performers. They saw me as a high performer or they wouldn't have hired me. I wanted to guard that."

Ned turned toward Tyler. "That's interesting. You hear that?"

Tyler thought for a moment. "Hear what?"

"You wanted to *guard* something. What's that sound like?"

Tyler considered the question. "*Guarding* is a lot like *protecting*, the first corner of your triangle."

Ned nodded.

"Why did I care? What was so worth guarding?"

Ned didn't answer.

"I'm a confident guy. I don't need their approval."

"Everybody wants the respect of their peers. There's nothing wrong with that."

"I suppose so, but I certainly went to extremes to protect it."

They walked to the edge of the twelfth tee. "To disappoint people, or frustrate people, especially people whose respect we want, puts us at risk," Ned said.

"I suppose it does. What was at risk?"

"Good question, what was at risk?"

Tyler considered his own question as the two men pulled out their clubs for their next drives. "I suppose some of it is phantom risk, to be honest. I felt more vulnerable than I actually was."

"I like that. Phantom risk. We fear things we don't need to fear."

"Yes, but not all of it. There was real risk. Jim Cooper experienced it. He was thrown under the bus. He lost significant money and his job was at risk."

"So there was real pain associated with offending the people you wanted to please."

"Yes. I wanted their respect, because it seemed like my well-being was in their hands. And from a certain vantage point, they did have authority in my life and could make things pretty miserable."

"Very true."

"But you would say my well-being wasn't in their hands."

"Actually, if you put your well-being into their hands, then it very well might have been. I'd suggest you not put your well-being into their hands. Putting your well-being into their hands is giving them god-like status in your life."

"So dropping a new ball and fixing my warped form has something to do with determining my source of protection."

"I'd suggest you get very clear about that. Lack of clarity puts you at risk of putting your well-being into the hands of somebody unqualified for the job. I've never met Tom Phelps, but from what you tell me, I'd not want my well-being in his hands. If I were to work with him, and we all work with the likes of him from time to time, I'd want to carry a strong sense of where my well-being truly rests."

Tyler swung his club back and forth just above the grass. "I get it. I need to process that, but I get it."

"That's good. Don't let me convince you of anything."

Ned paused.

"Let me suggest a second important question. Protection is just one corner of the triangle. A second question gets after at least one of the others, possibly both."

Ned wiped his hands on his towel.

"It's a simple question, but for most it takes a little processing, so pay attention to your reflex answer, but don't be surprised if you have to dig a little deeper. "Put simply, what do you want?"

Tyler wiped his club with his towel and looked toward Ned. "What do I want?"

"Yes, what do you want? What are you after? Why are you doing what you're doing?"

Tyler's forehead wrinkled. "I know that question," he said, "I've asked it many times."

Which brought back a memory.

He'd not thought about it in years.

He wasn't sure where it would lead, but it was a starting point and something about it made Tyler sense it held promise.

The Twelfth Hole

THE twelfth hole was a par three with a small lake on the right side of the green that came down and into the fairway just past two sand traps. Both men held their nine irons.

"So I'm seventeen years old," Tyler began. "In six months, I'll be off to college. It's a late Friday night. Blake and I, along with a few other friends, are lying on blankets at the end of a runway watching airplanes pass above us. We all know that in a matter of months we'll each head our own way in life. Doug, the more thoughtful of the bunch, poses a question. We all have to answer it. He asks us what we want to be true of us when we all return for our twentieth reunion," Tyler paused. "It's your *What do you want?* question in a slightly different form."

Ned positioned his ball.

"I didn't know what to say, so I spent most of the time listening. Blake knew his dream. He'd be a doctor but not your typical doctor. He'd practice medicine in a third world country where he was truly needed."

Ned grimaced as his shot landed in a sand trap fifteen yards in front of the green.

Tyler placed his ball.

"Angie, another good friend of ours, gushed a long list of dreams. Most of all, she wanted to have her own interior design company, which made perfect sense to all of us. She's highly creative. She also talked about family. She wanted five kids, two that she'd have herself and three she'd adopt out of some sort of impoverished situation. We all laughed thinking about Angie managing the chaos of five kids, considering she brings enough chaos of her own. We used to joke about it, but it's become a bit more sensitive as time goes on and she hasn't married."

Tyler paused for his drive, placing his ball on the fringe of the green.

"Doug was all about social action. He rattled off a couple causes he wanted to go after. Nobody was surprised by this. He's a great guy who genuinely wants a better world."

The two men picked up their bags and began the walk down the fairway.

"I was last to share. I waited in silence for a long time. I finally told them I wanted to be an Olympic gymnast."

Ned smiled. "Were you a gymnast?"

"Not at all. They all laughed. What I didn't tell them, though, was that as a kid that really is what I wanted to do. I begged my parents to let me join a gymnastics club, but they couldn't swing it financially. After the jokes subsided on the blanket, I told them I wanted to go into business. I didn't know what I'd do specifically, but I told them I wanted to make money. What I didn't tell them is why."

Tyler looked toward Ned.

"If you think about it, I bet you could guess my reason."

Ned walked silently. As they neared the green he pulled his sand wedge. He rested his bag at the edge of the green and stepped into the sand. He remained quiet as he lined up for his shot. His shot sprayed sand in front of him, and his ball landed on the green and rolled to the opposite side of the pin. Finally, he raked the sand and turned toward Tyler.

"Because you wanted to be a parent who could afford gymnastics lessons for your kids."

Tyler nodded as he walked toward his ball. His shot landed a bit closer to the pin than Ned's shot but out of the way.

"I knew I sounded materialistic, but I didn't care and didn't want to explain myself. I wondered if I might make enough money to fund Blake's third world medical practice, help Angie start her interior design business and adopt a few kids, or contribute to whatever cause Doug was championing. I didn't say all that, but I thought it. I wanted to make a pile of money and empower the lives of people I cared about. If I ever had kids, my kids would have the resources to fund their dreams."

"Has any of that happened?"

"Not so much. I've made good money, but by the time I'd done so, money wasn't what they needed, or I would have given it to them. I actually offered to help Blake get out of his suburban practice and into a third world country, but he was reluctant for other reasons. Angie already had her interior design practice going, although it wasn't all she hoped it would be. And Doug was more on the political lobbyist track than the social action track and was fully funded through other means, although I've made a few minor contributions."

Ned lined up for his putt. "So you wanted to make money, and you wanted to do good with that money. Is that it? Is that what you want?"

Ned's putt ringed the hole and rolled downhill back toward the sand trap.

"It's what I wanted at one time. I honestly don't know what I want now."

Tyler lined up and sank his putt for par.

"It just doesn't excite me as it once did," Tyler said. "I can get another job, and will no doubt do so in time, but I can't imagine I'll have the drive I once did."

Both men remained silent as Ned bent down and eyed the green for his second putt. Ned then stood, lined up for his putt, and made the shot.

"That's interesting," Ned said.

"What's interesting? That I've lost my mojo and have no drive?"

"Yes, it's interesting. Don't misunderstand what I'm going to say here—every single one of us is unique—but it never ceases to intrigue me how predictable it all is. You're a unique person with a unique contribution to make. But humanity does have a great deal that unites us, not the least of which is our deeply seated desires."

Tyler pulled the balls out of the hole and replaced the pin.

"I have an observation I want you to consider. I call it the bicycle observation, but before we go there, you need the third point on the triangle."

Tyler gently tossed Ned his ball.

"Any guesses to what the third point of the triangle would be? What's a deep desire of humanity not fully addressed by protection or purpose?"

Both men walked toward their bags. "So the points on the triangle are reflective of our deep desires," Tyler said. "How we satisfy those desires varies from person to person, but you're saying the desires themselves unite us."

"I am."

"I'd also suspect you've found a way to capture the essence of that third point of the triangle with the letter 'P.'"

"You can decide whether it works or not."

"If I think about desires not covered by *purpose* or *protection*, I can't help but think about happiness. Yes, I want to guard my well-being, and I want some sort of purpose. Much of my life has been about fun, though. I'm a bit of a thrill-chaser." Tyler lifted his bag to his shoulder.

"If I had to put that into a word that starts with a 'P' I'd probably go with *pleasure*."

"Yes, that's it. And I hope you see the simplicity in this. I also hope you see the depth, though. Our pursuit of pleasure is more than a pursuit of ice cream or slice of cake, although it certainly includes those things. It's a deep desire that propels a great deal of our lives. We don't just want *purpose* and *protection*. We want satisfaction—deep satisfaction—in life. When we win in business, for example, we feel good because it touches both *purpose* and *protection*, but it's also gratifying because winning feels good. There's a pleasure in it."

The two men turned down a slight hill toward the thirteenth tee.

"But we want even more than that. We want comfort, for example. Even if our tastes aren't extravagant, we prefer comfort to discomfort and work to provide it. Then there's our pursuit of beauty and joy. Why do we go to the beach or to the mountains? It's not typically about *purpose* or *protection*. Typically, it's about *pleasure*. We want to feast our eyes on something beautiful. We want to wade through blue water or slide down snow-powdered mountains. The pursuit of pleasure is a deep desire that drives us. It's an important part of what it means to be human."

"So my desire to fund my friend's dreams, which of these three desires was at play?"

"Good question. What do you think?"

Tyler looked away toward a distant collection of trees. "I can certainly see purpose. It feels purposeful to make a difference in the life of another person."

"I'd agree with that."

"But I can also see a degree of protection and pleasure in it as well. I'm protecting the people I love. I'm taking pleasure in seeing them satisfied."

"That's good. I like it."

Their walk slowed as they neared the thirteenth tee.

"So why have I backed off? Why don't I have the drive I once did?"

"I suppose there's a lot that could be said to that, but at a minimum, it brings us to the bicycle observation."

Tyler looked toward Ned. "Let me guess; it has something about *balance* and *momentum*. I've lost my drive because I've been out of balance."

"You've guessed well on a lot, but that's not what this is about," Ned said as he pointed toward the tee box. "Balance and momentum are good, but this one's a little less obvious than that."

The Thirteenth Hole

TYLER lined up for what he hoped would be a solid drive. The thirteenth hole was a long par four. He got the distance but was a bit off center.

As Ned positioned his ball, he asked a question. "Did you have a bicycle as a kid?"

Tyler waited to answer as Ned's shot bounced just shy of Tyler's.

"Yes, I had a bike. I had a couple of hand-me-downs from cousins in my very young years, but I picked up a paper route when I was eleven and made enough to buy the bike I really wanted."

"Any idea where that bike is?" Ned asked.

Tyler swung his bag over his shoulder and looked toward the

green. "No idea. I don't recall ever selling it, but I seriously doubt it's in my parents' garage. I suspect they got rid of it at some point."

"You're probably right." Ned picked up his bag and the two men began the walk down the fairway.

"Years ago," Ned said, "literally a couple of decades, I was visiting my mother not long before she passed. I was rummaging through her garage and found my childhood bike. It was a red Schwinn. You'd call it an antique now. Not unlike you, I worked for that bike. I'd seen it in the local bike shop and wanted it badly. Rather than buy it for me, my parents saw an opportunity to teach me the value of work. I mowed yards all summer and made enough money to buy that bike. It was a thrill."

Ned lifted his hat as they walked out of the sun and into the shade.

"So here's my question. Why did we lose interest in our bikes? And don't say the obvious. We didn't just outgrow them, because we didn't just lose interest in our *bikes*. We lost interest in riding altogether. Maybe we ride bikes every now and then, but not like we used to. Why?"

Tyler considered the question. "I suppose bicycles were replaced by cars in my world. I haven't really thought about it."

"That's true in part, but there's more to it than that. Riding a bike, even now, can be a pleasure, but it's not like it was as a kid. As a kid, it was a thrill. What changed?"

Tyler adjusted his bag on his shoulder. "That bicycle was a thrill at one time, but for whatever reason, it lost its attraction for me, and I moved on to other things. Maybe I moved on to cars or to girls or to who knows what. But your point is that the thrill of the bicycle didn't last forever."

"You're moving in the right direction. When I found my old bicycle I put it in my car and took it home with me. My wife was a bit less than thrilled until I explained why I wanted it. It now hangs on the back wall of my garage so I see it every time I pull in. I wanted it as a reminder."

"A reminder of the good old days?" Tyler said.

"No, a reminder of the *law of diminishing returns.*"

Tyler looked toward Ned with a slight squint in his eyes. "Isn't that an economics principle?"

"I see business school wasn't lost on you. Do you recall what it means?" Ned rested his bag and pulled his three wood.

"It's been awhile. I think it has something to do with more not always being better."

"That's right. If I own a bakery, two bakers will produce more than one baker, and three bakers will produce more than two bakers, but at some point if I add another baker, they're going to get in the way of each other, and another baker isn't going to add value."

"That's right," Tyler said. "I think I heard it explained in the context of farming. If a farmer adds fertilizer he grows more crops. If he keeps adding more fertilizer, though, at some point additional fertilizer is harmful."

"You got it. That's the law of diminishing returns. And my old bike reminds me of it every day."

"And how's that?"

Ned walked to the side of his ball and lined up for his shot. His ball bounced and rolled to the fringe at the upper side of the green.

"Because riding that bike was a thrill. I loved it. The first time I rode it, my satisfaction level was off the charts. So what did I do? I rode it more. The second time I rode it was a thrill as well, and so was the third. In time, though, my satisfaction level was noticeably less than the first time I rode it. Just like that farmer's fertilizer not being as effective as the first application of it, my bike was less effective at delivering a thrill. In time, I'd ridden that bike so much it wasn't thrilling at all, but just a means of transportation. Ultimately, there were better ways to get around—like driving a car—and the bike got left behind altogether."

"So now it hangs in your garage. You wanted the reminder for a reason. Why?"

Ned didn't respond as Tyler pulled his three iron and rested his bag. His shot landed pitching distance from the green. Tyler expected Ned to answer after he placed his club back in the bag, but he didn't.

Tyler finally spoke. "You obviously don't have that bike there to remind you about bikes. You have it hanging in your garage, because you wanted it for a more general reminder. It's not just bikes that deliver diminishing returns over time. Other things in life do so as well. I suppose you could say the same thing for our first cars. I'm not really a car guy, but my first car was a bit of a thrill. I don't think about cars hardly at all now. I just drive them."

Tyler looked toward Ned. "What else is subject to the law of diminishing returns?"

"What isn't?"

Tyler pulled his pitching wedge, swinging it by his side as he walked.

"I suppose you have a point. Most everything seems subject to it. I can have a glass of wine, maybe two, and I feel good. But at some point another glass of wine makes me feel worse and not better. You could say the same for food. I eat a couple pieces of pizza, and they taste good, but if I eat the whole thing I feel sick. Same could be said for sex. Sex is more satisfying when you pace yourself. I don't know that I've ever used the phrase 'too much sex,' but I certainly enjoy sex more when I don't obsess over it."

Tyler looked toward Ned, "I suppose you brought this up to apply it to my work."

Ned nodded, "I suppose you're right. How might you apply this observation to your work life?"

"Work is not the thrill it once was," Tyler said. "When I think back to that initial start-up years ago, we were riding downhill with the wind in our hair. It was hard work, but it was a thrill. I'll get another job again, but I can't imagine it will ever feel like that."

Tyler paused, giving thought to his words.

"I'm warming up to your bicycle observation. I'm not entirely sure what to do with it, though."

"What do you think you should do with it?"

Tyler rested his bag and walked to the side of his ball.

"I suppose I could go a couple of directions with it."

Tyler lined up for his shot and kept talking.

"On the one hand, I could leave a job behind like I left that bike behind, once the thrill wears off. I'd basically go from job to job."

Tyler's shot bounced and rolled toward the hole, coming to a stop about three feet from the pin.

"Or, I could adjust my expectations of what work is going to be like and just embrace it for what it is."

"That's good. How might you decide which of those two options you'd take?"

"I suppose there's not one answer to that question. For my bike, it was probably a good thing I moved on. It would be a little odd if I was into riding that bike like I was when I was a kid. But other things don't seem to work that way. If I had to change jobs every time the thrill wore off, I'd get nowhere in my career."

Ned looked toward Tyler. "Let's look at it from another angle. Let me see your wallet and your phone."

"You want my wallet and my phone?"

"Yes, let me see them both for a moment."

"Okay," Tyler said with a quizzical look on his face.

Ned first opened the wallet and rummaged through the various pockets. He finally pulled out a little slip of paper.

"I think this is it. It says, 'Tracy' and has a phone number. Is this the gal you met on the running trail?"

"That's her."

"Great," Ned said while sliding open Tyler's phone.

"What are you doing?" Tyler asked.

"I'm sending Tracy a text."

Tyler's eyebrows raised.

A few moments later, Ned read his typed text aloud, "Tracy, this is Tyler O'Brien. We met on the jogging trail a couple of times and then bumped into each other in the coffee shop. I'm an idiot for not calling. I have a few excuses, but they're weak. I wonder if you'd be willing to catch up for coffee sometime next week?"

"Not bad," Tyler said. "I don't know that I'd have called myself an idiot, but I like the humble approach. Go ahead and send it."

"I already did," Ned said as he walked toward his ball on the upper fringe.

"Now here's my question," Ned said. "Let's say Tracy responds positively. And let's say you catch up next week. And let's say that first coffee goes great, and ultimately the relationship turns into something. What are you going to do when the thrill wears off?"

"Wait a minute. You sent the text without first reading it to me?"

Ned lined up for his shot, putting from the fringe. "Up until a couple of holes ago I was calling you Dr. Hill, so don't get too worked up."

Tyler smiled, "You have a point."

Ned's putt rolled to a stop between the hole and Tyler's ball.

"And my question stands. What are you going to do when the thrill wears off?"

Tyler didn't answer as Ned moved his ball and placed a ball marker.

"So how do you do it, Ned? How do you keep from jumping ship every time the thrill wears off, whether it be a job, a relationship, or something else?"

Ned returned the question with a question, "You mentioned wine. How might you do this with wine?"

Tyler lined up and sank his putt.

"To be truthful, I don't always do too well with wine. I think I get where you're going, though. The person who handles wine well is the person who knows when the next glass is going to be harmful rather than helpful, just like that farmer knows when another layer of fertilizer is going to be harmful rather than helpful. If you learn where the law of diminishing returns kicks in, you know when to stop."

"That's good," Ned said as he placed his ball on the green and picked up his marker. "But what if you don't know when to stop? Or worse, what if you do know when to stop but don't have the self-control to do it?"

Tyler raised his eyebrows. "That's when you have a problem."

"That's right," Ned said as his putt dropped in the hole, "which is the limitation of the bicycle observation. It highlights a problem but doesn't give a solution. Over the years I've given the problem a name. I've labeled it *groping*. I don't mean that in the sexual sense, although it certainly applies to that. I mean it to describe our persistent groping for more. You and I, we're tough to satisfy. The bicycle observation highlights this. We're not content with that bicycle, so we grope for more. We're not content with a certain amount of money, so we grope for more. We're not content with our job, so we grope for another job. We're not content with a romantic relationship, so we grope for a new one. We're not content with a single plate of food, so we grope for more. There's something about the human condition. We consistently want more than we have."

"So what's it take? What do you do with that?"

"What do you do with it?" Ned returned the question.

Tyler picked up his bag and walked toward Ned. "To date, I think I've simply given into it. I've just moved on to the next thing, and once the thrill is gone, the next thing. I guess I'm a thrill-seeker."

"To a certain degree, we all are." Ned picked up his bag and the two men walked toward the next tee. "Not as thrill-seeking is commonly understood; we don't all want to jump out of airplanes. But we all do seek satisfaction, and pleasure, and purpose, and we seek for ways to protect ourselves. And it's not at all uncommon for whatever degree we have obtained these things, for them to not feel quite enough."

As Tyler rolled the thoughts through his mind, he quietly lifted his phone to see if Tracy had responded. She hadn't.

"Any response from Tracy?" Ned noticed Tyler's glance to his phone.

"Not yet."

"Not yet. I like your optimism."

She'll respond, Tyler thought. There was something about it, like it was meant to be.

"Let me show you something." Ned pulled out their scorecard. "To better understand how I've wrestled with this groping as I've called it, I need to make a distinction."

Ned drew the triangle on the back of the scorecard, and next to the lower right corner he wrote the word *pleasure* two times: *pleasure* and *PLEASURE*. He did the same with each of the corners: *protection* and *PROTECTION*, *purpose* and *PURPOSE*.

"What's the distinction?" Tyler asked.

"It's a distinction of ultimate versus penultimate, or if you want to use simpler language, primary versus secondary."

Tyler nodded, curious where Ned was going.

"Consider ice cream. Is ice cream the ultimate pleasure, ultimate satisfaction, or is it a secondary satisfaction, something you enjoy but not something you live for?"

"I'd call it secondary or penultimate," Tyler said.

"That's good. It's a simple one. How about riding that bike as a kid? Primary or secondary? Ultimate or penultimate?"

"It might have felt ultimate at the time, but I suppose it wasn't. I suppose it's more like ice cream. It's something I enjoyed, but it wasn't my ultimate pleasure in life."

"That's good again, so how are you making the distinction? You've pretty easily named two things penultimate. What would it take for something to be ultimate?"

Tyler looked down the next fairway and pulled his driver. Ned put the scorecard back in his pocket.

"I don't really know, but I suspect..."

Tyler's phone vibrated. He couldn't help but pause and lift it up.

"It's from Tracy," Tyler said, almost to himself.

Did I see you in the golf pro-shop this morning?

Tyler's eyes darted toward Ned who was pulling his driver. His mind raced back to his quick pass through the clubhouse. He vaguely recalled someone off to the side but he hadn't seen her face.

Yes, you were there?

Tyler waited as Ned wiped his driver with a towel.

It sounded like you, and looked like you from the side, but the guy called you Dr. Hill? What's that about?

The guy behind the counter, Tyler remembered. He'd referred to him as Dr. Hill.

Long story. Too much for text but would love to explain over coffee. What were you doing there? You play golf?

Tyler watched his phone as he rummaged for a tee.

I play some but not today. I was dropping my grand-father off. Needed to borrow his car.

Tyler's eyes darted toward Ned. Grandfather? Surely not. The course was surprisingly empty, but there were other candidates out there who could be her grandfather.

"She respond positively?" Ned asked.

Tyler stared at his phone.

"I think so. We'll see," Tyler said as he typed another text.

"You can thank me later."

Tyler nodding slowly.

"Yes. I can." Tyler mumbled quietly. "And I suspect I will."

The Fourteenth Hole

THE fourteenth hole had it all. Not only was it a par five, but it had water on the south side of the fairway, a short dogleg just before the green, and an unusual collection of three sand traps midway to the hole. Unquestionably, it was the toughest hole on the course.

Ned placed a solid drive.

Tyler placed his tee, and took a practice swing. Clearly his mind was not on his game. His drive sailed past the bunkers and landed near Ned's ball, well-placed and midway to the green.

They picked up their bags and began the walk. Ned remained silent, letting Tyler pick up the conversation when he was ready.

"So what's ultimate?" Tyler finally asked.

"That's a big question," Ned said. "Switch categories for a moment. We kicked it around a bit with the pleasure category. Move back to protection. What might be ultimate or penultimate means for our protection and well-being?"

Tyler pulled his three wood and swung it by his side as he walked and thought.

"To answer that," Tyler said, "I suppose I'd go with the obvious here. What gives me ultimate protection in life and what gives me some sort of secondary protection in life?"

"That's good. You're getting the distinction."

"Based on our conversation earlier, I suspect you'd say God gives you ultimate protection. Thinking back to the David and Goliath story, David seemed to look to God to be his ultimate protection."

"That's true. What did he look to for his penultimate or secondary protection?"

Tyler put his three wood back and pulled his three iron. "I suppose his sling or his skill with the sling."

"That's good. I think you're right. He looked to God as his ultimate protector, but that didn't mean he didn't pick up a sling and a handful of rocks. There was some sort of interplay between his primary and secondary protection. Now play that out. What were the other Israelite warriors looking to for ultimate protection?"

Tyler's three iron swung by his side as they walked. "I suppose they looked at their own skills and weapons as if they were ultimate, but because they knew they were inadequate, they feared for their lives."

"That's good again. They couldn't get their eyes off themselves. They themselves, with their weapons, were their ultimate protection. They might have said otherwise had you asked them, but that's what their actions revealed."

The two men slowed their walk as they neared the first ball. Ned pulled his three wood and walked to the side of his ball. Both men remained silent as Ned's shot rolled a hundred yards shy of the green.

"So let's go back to that groping question," Ned said. "Why might those Israelite warriors grope for more protection?"

The two men walked toward Tyler's ball.

"I suppose because when you instinctively know you're vulnerable, you want more."

Ned nodded. "When you hear the story of David and Goliath, do you hear any groping with David?"

"I don't know the details of the story, but not from what I do know."

"It's actually quite interesting. They tried to give David armor, but he refused. He couldn't walk well in it, so he took it off and just took his sling and the rocks. It's as if he did the opposite of groping for more. He reduced his secondary protection to only that which suited him. I'm convinced the only reason he could do this was because his primary protection was well in place."

Tyler set his bag down and walked toward his ball. "So how does that apply to my world?"

"I'm more interested in what you think. How do you think it applies? Or do this, you answered the 'what's our ultimate protection' question by turning it back to me, saying I'd say God is my ultimate protector. But what do you say? What have you looked to for ultimate protection?"

Tyler lined up for his shot as he considered Ned's question. His ball landed just beyond Ned's but not by much.

"Business skills are my slingshot...and money I suppose. I protect myself in other ways, though. I do my best to eat well and exercise."

"That's good. Would you call those primary or secondary protection?"

Tyler lifted his bag as the two men began walking. "The distinction's new to me. I don't really know how to answer. But when I ask if these things are my ultimate protection in life, that seems a bit of an overstatement. I then think about recent events in my work, though, and how I didn't take a stand sooner." Tyler paused, "If I'm honest about my ultimate protection, I'd say I look to myself. A more irritating thought, though, is that maybe I looked to Tom Phelps and others as if they held my ultimate well-being in their hands. I don't want to think too much about that. It'll ruin my game."

"That's good. Very honest. I get it and won't press it, but don't lose that thought. All of us are susceptible to treat a secondary authority, like Tom or the board, as if they're primary. It's understandable, because they do have real authority in our lives and can affect our well-being. They don't have ultimate authority, though, and they don't hold our ultimate well-being. The more I've internalized God as my ultimate authority, the less susceptible I've been to allowing a person to have too much sway in my life."

Tyler nodded.

"You mentioned money. How have you looked to money as a protector?"

Tyler pulled his nine iron as they walked. "I'm not greedy, but I do like to make money. I like to fully maximize life's experiences. Money funds that. If I'm understanding you correctly, you're saying when we take something that's secondary, and treat it like it's primary, that's when we grope for more."

"You got it."

"Seems a little demotivating when I apply that to money. I get what you're saying, but right or wrong, I like my drive. If money gets demoted, do you idle back?"

"I like that question. My response would be that it depends upon your perspective, but I'd prefer you to wrestle that out. If we're no longer driven by the tainted fuel of attempting to make money something it's not, what drives us then?"

Tyler considered the question as Ned pulled his nine iron and walked to the side of his ball. Ned's shot bounced on the green to the left of the pin by about ten yards.

"We still need money," Tyler said, "so no doubt we're motivated to work and make a good living."

Tyler walked toward his ball and rested his bag.

"At some point, I know more money won't provide greater protection, though, so why do I keep at it?" Tyler walked to the side of his ball. "I suppose it has something to do with one of your other two corners, pleasure or purpose. I'm no longer increasing my paycheck because I need to provide for myself, but in my world, money is a scoreboard. It's satisfying to rack up points. I guess that means part of my drive for money is the pleasure of the win. There are other ways to define a win but money is a tangible way, and I don't think that's all bad."

"I get it and agree. It's satisfying to win in anything, and in certain lines of work, money is evidence of a win. Take that thought, though, and apply the ultimate versus penultimate question with regards to money in the pleasure category."

Tyler's ball rolled to a stop near Ned's.

"At some point," Tyler said, "the pursuit of financial gain becomes a treadmill." Tyler placed his nine iron in his bag. "It provides protection, it provides the pleasure of a win, but at some point you weary of the chase, and it's not what it used to be."

"The law of diminishing returns," Ned said. "That moment—when the pursuit of money becomes a treadmill—that's the glass of wine that gives a headache rather than relaxes you. It's that moment when we realize our pursuit of financial gain is no longer giving us life but taking life away from us. We don't need more money for protection, and it's no longer pleasurable to work so hard for it. So the protection corner and the pleasure corner no longer drive us, which leaves us with the purpose corner and the inevitable question we all ask."

"Why?" Tyler said.

"That's it. Why am I doing this? What's the purpose? I'm knocking myself out to increase my bottom-line. It doesn't seem to serve a purpose. What's the point?"

"I've asked that question many times," Tyler said as he rested his bag.

"We all have, and it's a good question."

"How have you answered it?" Tyler asked.

Ned paused before responding as Tyler walked over to his ball, placed a ball marker, and picked the ball up to be out of Ned's way.

"You ever thought much about the word *provision*?" Ned said.

Ned grimaced as his putt rolled seemingly over the hole.

"I haven't." Tyler placed his ball next to his ball marker.

"It's a fascinating word. We think about it with regards to food and shelter, our provision for life. But pull that word apart. It actually points to quite a bit more than life's necessities."

"How so?"

"You have *pro* and you have *vision*. That little word *pro* is actually quite powerful. It means 'for.'"

Tyler thought for a moment, "For vision."

Ned nodded. "It's a powerful way to look at money. When we say it's provision, we're saying its purpose is to fund the fulfillment of a vision."

"Which is important when we ask the 'why' question," Tyler said as he lined up for his putt.

"Incredibly important. Money itself is not a vision. It's a means to fulfill a vision." Ned paused as Tyler's putt rolled toward the hole, stopping less than a foot from dropping.

"Go ahead and finish out," Ned said.

Tyler lined up and sank the short putt.

"One of the great tragedies of humanity is we mix this up," Ned said. "We treat money as if it's the vision itself. Money is a means to an end. If you don't have a vision for what you're going to do with money, or if that vision gets fulfilled, the pursuit of more money leaves us disillusioned with it."

"Or if you increase your vision," Tyler said, "it can take on an entirely new purpose."

"That's correct. Internalize that and you're onto something. It's why we kick over to the purpose corner and ask 'Why?' Our initial vision for finances is often about protection and pleasure. We want to provide for ourselves and our loved ones, and we want to enjoy some of the things we can do with money. That's all good. But the law of diminishing returns kicks in at some point. More money no longer gives more protection or more pleasure. If you don't have a vision from the purpose corner, motivation dries up."

Tyler thought for a moment, "Your work against sex trafficking, is that your ultimate purpose?"

Ned eyed the green for his putt. "You're asking the right question. To be sure, that work in establishing these safe houses certainly motivates my wife and me to think about how we manage our money. We have a vision for freeing these women from oppression. That vision needs provision, and we're very mindful of that. It's incredibly rewarding—and yes, purposeful—to direct our resources toward that cause. With that said, though, it's not my ultimate purpose. It's penultimate."

Tyler looked toward Ned. "That kind of surprises me. I would think a cause like that would be ultimate."

Ned lined up for his putt, about two yards from the hole. His ball ringed the hole and dropped.

"It's profoundly important, as many secondary purposes are, but it's not ultimate."

"So what's ultimate for you in the purpose category?"

Ned walked to the hole, bent over, and retrieved their balls. Tyler picked up the pin and placed it in the hole.

Ned didn't answer immediately as the two men picked up their bags and walked toward the next tee.

Ned posed a question as the two men walked. "Do you like french fries?"

Tyler looked toward Ned without responding.

"How about sweet potato fries? Do you like those?"

"I do," Tyler said.

"I discovered my ultimate purpose through a plate of sweet potato fries."

Tyler was going to ask a further question but was interrupted by the vibration of his phone. He was waiting for a response to a question he'd posed to Tracy and couldn't resist pulling the phone from his pocket.

YES!!! Are you seriously playing golf with him?

The day just took a turn Tyler certainly didn't expect.

The Fifteenth Hole

THE fifteenth hole was tree-lined par four. Tyler was silent as he lined up for his drive. His ball rolled to a stop about a hundred yards shy of the green.

"So let's go for it here. Let's ask the big question," Ned said as he placed his tee into the ground. "What's your purpose? Why are you here?"

"Evidently to eat sweet potato fries." Tyler slid his driver into his bag.

"We'll get there in a moment," Ned said. "Why are you here? What's your purpose?"

Tyler considered the question as Ned's shot sailed down the center of the fairway. The last time he remembered really considering that question was in a café in Amsterdam. He'd fallen into a conversation with a Rastafarian from Jamaica. It was a wild conversation, one he'd never forget.

"Years ago," Tyler said as Ned's ball rolled to a stop, "I had a late night conversation on this very question with a guy in Amsterdam."

Ned put his driver away and lifted his bag to his shoulder.

"It was a lively conversation. We had a great time. I was a bit surprised by my own conclusions. I didn't even know if I agreed with them. I don't think the guy I was talking to agreed with them, but it made for good conversation."

Tyler looked toward Ned.

"In your language, I combined two of the corners. I decided that ultimate purpose had something to do with pleasure, which sounds trivial. Shouldn't our purpose be about making a difference in this world? I argued, though, that all of our efforts to make the world a better place are an effort to increase people's pleasure. We want war to end, so pleasure can be restored. We want to liberate people from oppression, because we want people to enjoy their lives. I didn't have it all worked out and obviously wasn't using your language at the time, but it seemed to me that pleasure had something to do with purpose."

"There's something quite profound in what you're saying."

"An experience I had not long after that made me question it all."

"How so?"

"I'd spent a little over three years living mostly in Amsterdam. I got restless, though, and heard the Grecian islands were a good spot. I scoped out a little island, Santorini. That island delivered. It was amazing. But after three months of being there, I was sitting on a high rock overlooking one of the beaches, and I said something, almost audibly, that surprised me."

Tyler paused remembering the moment.

"I said, 'This isn't it.'"

Tyler looked toward Ned. "I surprised myself when I said that. It's not like I was consciously looking for something. But almost out of nowhere I whispered to myself, 'This isn't it.' I haven't thought much about that moment since then, but I do recall questioning my *pleasure is my purpose* conclusion. I was experiencing some of life's greatest pleasures, but there I was instinctively saying, 'This isn't it.'" Tyler squinted from a burst of sunlight coming through the trees. "That might have been the moment I decided to come back home."

"You expected more."

"I did. I'd thought I might finally be happy—not having to work and all—but despite the most amazing time a person could ever have, I wasn't. I was still searching, and I didn't even realize it. I'd never said I was going to be on any sort of quest. I was just living my life. Then there I was, looking out over the most amazing view you could ever imagine, and I said to myself, 'This isn't it.'"

Ned nodded.

Tyler expected Ned to say more, but he didn't. As they neared Ned's ball, Tyler finally asked, "So what's with sweet potato fries?"

Ned placed his bag and pulled his six iron. "Years ago my wife and kids were out of town visiting her parents. I had the weekend to myself, which was fine, but I'd had a particularly hard week. I didn't want to be alone with my thoughts, so I decided to make myself busy. I went to the store, bought items for a steak dinner—including sweet potatoes—and came home with the intention of getting lost in the making of a somewhat elaborate dinner."

Ned lined up for his shot. His ball rolled to the side of the green, between the fringe and a large sand trap.

"As I was making the dinner, I started a conversation with God. Call it prayer if you'd like. An outsider would have thought I was talking to myself. I was talking to God about my frustrations. Finally, I got through my list of frustrations and asked God a question."

Ned placed his iron back in his bag.

"I asked why he created me."

The two men walked toward Tyler's ball.

"As I let the question hang in the air, I liked it. It was a fresh angle on the '*What's my purpose in life?*' question, which was closely related to why I was frustrated. It all seemed so meaningless. I was working terribly hard, and it just seemed like a treadmill. I wanted to know why he created me. I reasoned that when I create something, I create it with a purpose. If I build a house or a car, that house or car has a purpose. If I build a boat, that boat has a purpose. Understanding why a person creates something helps us understand the purpose of whatever has been created."

Tyler nodded.

"As the question is hanging in the air, I'm slicing sweet potatoes for sweet potato fries. As I'm dropping the slices into a pan of boiling olive oil, a question comes to mind."

Ned looked toward Tyler.

"'Why are you making the sweet potato fries?'

"I realize that sounds odd, but it didn't seem odd at the time. It seemed important. I thought about it for a moment, and I finally answered, 'Because I like sweet potato fries. I'm making them, because I want to enjoy them.'"

Ned slowed as they neared Tyler's ball.

"Those fries, if they were to ask me, their creator, what their purpose was, I would have said their purpose in life was to be enjoyed by their creator."

Tyler pulled his nine iron.

"The next thought fell into place rather easily. I couldn't help but consider if God's purpose in creating me was to enjoy me. He certainly didn't need me. If he truly is God, he's not in need of me to do anything for him. Which is good, because I'd rather be wanted than needed. I need lots of things, but that doesn't mean I want them. To be wanted is a higher honor."

Tyler lined up for his shot and placed his ball on the far side of the green.

"My mind then went to my kids, and a second question came to me. '*Why did you want to have kids?*' I thought about it for a moment, and I thought about those sweet potato fries. My answer was similar. I wanted kids, because I wanted to enjoy them. I wanted to relate to them. I didn't have kids so I could offload my weekly chore list. It wasn't that I needed somebody to mow my yard. I had kids because I wanted to know them and wanted them to know me. I wanted the joy of having a hand in their development, watching them grow into adults, having a relationship with them."

Tyler placed his iron back in his bag and the two men walked toward the green.

"So there I am, in my kitchen, thinking about sweet potato fries and my kids, and something clicks into place for me. I recalled the time in Scripture where they come to Jesus and ask him what's most important in all of Scripture. Without hesitating, Jesus tells them the most important command in all of Scripture is to love God with all your heart, soul, mind, and strength. He then says the second most important thing in all of Scripture is to love your neighbor as yourself. He pulled it together by saying that everything else in all of Scripture hangs on those two hooks. He might as well have said that all of life hangs on them. It all comes down to loving God and loving people. And as I was thinking about it while eating that meal, I swapped out the word *love* for the word *enjoy*."

"Why's that?"

Ned's walk slowed slightly. "Love is much broader than enjoy, but the word enjoy captured something I'd missed. The highest honor I can pay my wife is to enjoy her. I can love her by doing something for her, helping her with a project she needs help on for example. But it's when I want to be with her simply because I like her, not because she needs me or I need her, that I honor her most."

Tyler considered the thought. "And how does that work out with God?"

"I realized at a deeper level that night, that God created me—and all humanity I'm convinced—because he wanted a people he would enjoy and who would ultimately enjoy him. He didn't need us. He wanted us. That's better."

Tyler looked toward the green and then back toward Ned. "That reminds me of a thought I had when deciding to come home from Greece. I had the conscious thought that I'd like to bring my family back to that island one day, if I ever had a family."

"That's interesting. Tell me more."

"As great of a time as I was having, I wanted to share it with people I really cared about. And that's not to say I didn't care about the people I was meeting. They were great people. I just remember thinking, if I ever have a wife, or maybe a son or a daughter, I'm bringing them here. They've got to see this."

"So one of the reasons you might want to be a dad some day is you want to share life's experiences with a son or a daughter."

Tyler pulled his putter and swung it by his side.

"I suppose so. I don't think about the prospect of parenting much. I haven't had time to think about it. But it does seem like it would bring a new degree of meaning and purpose to most anything I was doing. Making money is good, but it would be more meaningful if I was using it to support a family. Being at that island was good, but at some point, I'd had enough and the only remaining thought was that if I had kids, I wanted to come back with them."

"If you have a daughter one day, you want to take her to Santorini, because you want to show her something beautiful. You love her, so you want her to see something good."

"Yes, something like that."

"Why do you think God might say, then, that the most important thing we could do with our lives is to love him? Why didn't he say the most important thing we could do with our lives is to love beaches in Santorini?"

Tyler reached for his towel dangling from his bag. "My daughter would love that beach, but like me, she'd tire of it eventually. Using your language, the law of diminishing returns would set in."

"So that's why he wouldn't say loving beaches in Santorini is the most important thing you can do with your life. Why would he say loving *him* is most important?"

Tyler dropped the towel back down to the side of his bag. "I don't honestly know. I can see how it sounds noble, especially when coupled with loving your neighbor, but it strikes me as odd."

"It does, I agree, but let me give you an intriguing thought that helped me a great deal on this."

Ned pulled his pitching wedge, rested his bag, and walked to the side of his ball.

"There's a profound portion of Scripture called Ecclesiastes. It's thousands of years old and is essentially the journal of a king named Solomon."

Ned's shot arched, landed on the green, rolled back toward the pin, and stopped about five feet from the hole.

"Solomon was a seeker of wisdom. The writings describe his quest for meaning and purpose in life. In his search, he tried everything. He had business ventures, intellectual pursuits, sexual encounters. He says he spared himself nothing his eyes desired. After experiencing it all, though, Solomon effectively said it all left him wanting."

"The law of diminishing returns," Tyler said.

"Yes, but what got my attention years ago was an observation Solomon made. If you read too quickly, you almost miss it. He said, 'God has placed eternity in people's hearts.' When I first read that years ago, I passed over it, and then jumped right back to it. It was a description of our hearts, the seat of our desires. I knew I had deep desire, deep hunger in my heart. I didn't realize it was an *eternal* desire. Knowing it was an eternal desire helped me understand why temporal experiences in life—like the world's best beaches—don't fully satisfy it. An eternal desire needs an eternal satisfaction for that desire. Scripture describes God as eternal."

"So an eternal desire is matched with an eternal object of our desire," Tyler said.

"Exactly. When we're taught the most important thing we could do with our lives is to love God, I like to describe this as enjoying God. With my kids, I wanted them to enjoy many things, and that beach in Santorini would certainly be on my list. But I also know that beach is limited. It can only deliver so much pleasure. It could satisfy my lowercase *pleasure*, but it won't satisfy my uppercase *PLEASURE*. This helps me understand why we might make God ultimate. Scripture's description of God as eternal captured my imagination. He's not limited. That beach is limited. Ice cream is limited. Jobs are limited. If God is eternal, he won't leave us wanting."

Tyler rested his bag at the edge of the green.

"Let me ask you a question. You mentioned taking your daughter to Santorini one day. Why not just send her there without you? Would that be the same?"

"Of course not," Tyler said as he walked around the edge of the green toward his ball. "There's something about the shared experience."

"Yes, if it was just about the beach, you might send her there alone. But it's more than that. It's about experiencing the beach together. You might even say that relating to each other is more important than relating to the beach and the beach simply provides a playground to do so."

Tyler lined up for his long putt. His ball caught slight slope in the green and came to a stop two feet to the right of the hole.

"I like that," Tyler said as Ned lined up for his putt, "a playground to enjoy each other."

Ned's putt ringed the hole and rolled two feet beyond the hole.

"So here's a thought. What if life is a playground designed for us to discover how to relate to God? What if it's not just about going to the beach for the sake of the beach? What if it's about who we go to the beach with?"

Tyler's putt dropped in the hole.

"That's the thought that captured my imagination and still does."

Ned lined up and sank his putt.

"What do you mean when you say that this thought of God captured your imagination?"

Tyler retrieved the pin and walked back toward the hole.

"I don't know that I can put this into words. This life—and all that it offers—it's just the beginning. I get a taste of God today, and there's something about my engagement with God that's deeply satisfying. But I also know this is just the beginning. That beach in Santorini, not only would I enjoy it, but if I were there, it would also excite expectation in me. I'd wonder what else God has created that I know nothing about yet. And I'd wonder about God himself, as the Creator of that beach and that island. I'd like to think I'm getting to know God as I walk through life with him, but if he's eternal, there's eternally more I've yet to discover about him. Life's a wonderful mystery and an adventure of discovering more of life and more of God. Recognizing this and experiencing this, it's put many things in their place."

"How so?"

Tyler handed Ned his ball as the two men walked back toward their bags.

"When we have what's most important in place, everything else lines up. Take work. When I finally let God be ultimate in my life, I was able to engage work in a good and healthy way. When God wasn't ultimate, I attempted to make work ultimate, which created a host of problems. Work is important—incredibly important—but it's not ultimate."

"So you demoted work?"

"You could say that, but demoting it created a perspective on work I didn't expect. When I let work take it's healthy place in my life, I enjoyed work more not less. The only way I can explain it is that I was finally able to enjoy work for what it is rather than hate it for what it's not. When I expected work to be my ultimate satisfaction, it failed at this and left me frustrated and disillusioned with all my efforts. When I let work be and do what it's capable of being and doing—delivering a degree of satisfaction but not ultimate satisfaction—I relaxed and enjoyed it."

"How about your performance?" Tyler asked. "I don't know if I make work ultimate in my life. I probably do. Demoting it might make me take it less seriously. I don't want to obsess over each month's profit and loss statement, but I also know I have to work incredibly hard to make it positive. If I don't treat it as ultimate, I might take it lightly and get terribly screwed."

"That's an important question." The two men walked toward the next tee box. "And what's fascinating, is that the effect has been the exact opposite."

"How so?"

"You ever hear a baseball coach tell a player he's squeezing the bat too hard? You squeeze the bat too hard, and you can't swing it. Same thing in golf. You squeeze the club too hard, and you can't swing it. Catching a glimpse—just a glimpse—of a greater grander vision, it's loosened my grip on life's daily realities in a positive not a negative way. When that P&L is ultimate, and when I obsess over it, it's not long before my white-knuckled grip ruins my ability to perform. I squeeze the club so hard I can't swing it and my drive lands in the next fairway. If you're going to win in business, you've got to swing the club and swing deliberately. This involves a great deal of hard work, periodic risks, and really going for it. The greater vision hasn't been a distraction from this life. It's actually giving me the ability to more fully engage."

As they turned a corner on the path, Tyler pulled out his phone.

"Ned, let's take a quick photo."

Ned looked at Tyler a little oddly. Tyler knew it was a bit abrupt, but he thought a selfie of him and Ned would be the best response to Tracy's text. Tyler held out his arm and snapped the photo, the two men barely stopping their walk toward the next tee.

"Tracy was a bit surprised I'm playing golf with her grandfather. I need the photo for proof."

Ned stopped walking.

Tyler remained silent as he attached the photo to a text and sent it to Tracy.

"It's okay, Ned. You don't need to worry. I'll back off. You know me too well. She's clearly above my pay grade."

Ned didn't respond but slowly resumed his walk.

"I'm sure she's a great gal. I'm clearly not cut out to date the granddaughter of a minister or pastor or whatever you're called."

"You've got to be kidding me," Ned finally said. "That Tracy?"

"That's the one."

A sly grin crossed Ned's face. He shook his head slowly.

"I even dialed her number. It's not like the good old days when you know a person's number. The only time I've seen that number is when I punched it into my phone and typed her name. That's been a few years."

"And it's a big city. Lots of Tracys."

"Yes, but you'd think I might have at least asked."

"You don't need to worry, Ned."

"No, actually...I'm not worried at all," Ned's voice trailed off.

Tyler knew Ned was absorbing this new development, and it'd be better to take it slow.

"Interesting," Ned said.

"How so?" Tyler finally asked.

"You don't know Tracy. I obviously know her well. This is very interesting...very interesting," he said almost under his breath.

Tyler didn't respond despite his curiosity for Ned's true thoughts.

"Interesting," Ned said again as he placed his bag next to a bench and pulled his driver.

The Sixteenth Hole

TYLER pushed his tee into the ground.

"This conversation just jumped a few levels in importance," Ned said.

Tyler lined up for his drive.

"That's not to say it wasn't important before. It was."

"I run into her around town two or three times. We're both a little intrigued. I disappear, unfortunately, but six months later I reappear playing golf with her grandfather. It is a little odd."

Tyler's drive sailed down the middle of the fairway.

"Maybe this happened today, Ned, because you're supposed protect her from me. Maybe your job today is to scare me off."

Ned didn't comment as his drive bounced and rolled just past Tyler's.

The two men picked up their bags and began the walk down the fairway.

Tyler's phone buzzed.

Nice! Ask him if I should have coffee with you.

Tyler smiled. "She suggested I ask you if she should have coffee with me."

"One of the wonderful things about Tracy," Ned said, "is that she's reached a point in her life when she genuinely wants my input, but she genuinely doesn't need it."

"Sounds healthy."

"It is. It hasn't always been that way. Tracy wouldn't at all be bothered if she heard me say it's been a good but rough road."

"How so?"

"Tracy has a beautiful story. She's been through a great deal, but it's a beautiful story. When you ran into her, did you ever meet her boy?"

"You mean Cooper, her dog?"

"No, Cooper's a good dog, but I mean her son." Ned said, "Other than my wife, Tracy and her son are—hands down—the best part of my life."

Tyler wasn't bothered by the fact that she had a son, but he instinctively knew Ned was still processing what was happening.

"When Tracy was sixteen, her dad, my son-in-law, died in a tragic car accident. That event sent her reeling. She left for college a little over a year later with a host of questions and doubts about all that had given her confidence. It's been a journey for her—and for us—but I couldn't be more proud of who she's become. She has a depth only found through hardship."

Tyler didn't know Tracy, but even this little information lined up with his brief encounter. She carried herself with a humble confidence that seemed beyond her years.

Tyler pulled his three wood. His shot dropped shy of the green by twenty yards.

"I think I'm a little intimidated," Tyler finally said.

"How so?"

Ned pulled his three wood as they walked toward his ball.

"Tracy sounds like a better person than me."

"She is."

"And I take no offense at your agreement with that."

Ned's shot landed fifteen yards to the left of Tyler's.

"That's interesting," Tyler said as Ned placed his club back in his bag.

"What's interesting?"

The two men walked slowly down the fairway.

"Your comment about a kind of depth that comes through hardship. Tell me about that."

Ned pulled his pitching wedge and wiped dirt off the end as they walked.

"You ever heard it said that almost all analogies break down if you push them too far?"

"I don't think so," Tyler said.

"I suggested a moment ago that life is like a playground designed for us to discover how to relate to God. We talked about going to the beach, not for the beach's sake, but for a place to relate to the people you love."

Tyler nodded.

"That analogy is good, I like it, but it also breaks down."

"How so?"

"What do you think? How might it break down?"

Tyler thought for a moment. Putting it alongside the few things he'd just heard about Tracy, he thought he knew where Ned was going.

"Life isn't all beaches and playgrounds," Tyler finally said.

"That's right. Life has its moments of beauty and joy, but it also has a great deal of hardship. Some of that hardship is extreme, like Tracy losing her dad at a tender time of life. Other aspects of life are the daily kind of hard, like you've experienced in your work."

Tyler took this in, not responding immediately, then asked, "What do you do with that?"

"You tell me. What do you do with it?" Ned asked back.

Tyler had dealt with hardship numerous ways. He'd responded to the hardship of his childhood by carving out a business career that would solve the problems of his early life. Other challenges he'd dealt with differently though. There were times he squared off with the hardship and other times he'd run from it.

"I don't have a single answer for that," Tyler finally said.

"That's good," Ned said. "Hardship brings about different responses at different times."

"Last week, I responded by snapping. Not sure I want to make a habit of that, though."

"Probably shouldn't. You won't get too far if you deliver repeat performances in other settings."

Tyler pulled his pitching wedge as they neared his ball.

"Think about the three corners of the triangle," Ned said. "Hardship could be described a lot of ways. In the context of this conversation, I'd describe it as when there is some sort of assault on one or more of those corners, those deep desires."

"How so?" Tyler asked.

"We desire protection, and something happens that hurts us. We desire pleasure, and something happens that's miserable. We desire purpose, and we're stuck in a season of aimlessness. You challenge any one of those corners, or worse, all corners at the same time, and you're experiencing hardship. How do you handle that? What do you do?"

"I drink," Tyler said with a smile.

Ned laughed. "You say that lightly, but you're onto something. One of our tendencies is to anesthetize the pain of hardship. We drink it away, or eat it away, or lean into some other escapist behavior."

"No doubt some of that can be destructive," Tyler said, "but don't you think some of that's normal. We could all use a little comfort food now and then, or a glass of wine after a hard day, don't you think?"

"I'm more interested in what you think."

Tyler rested his bag and walked to the side of his ball. His shot rolled to a stop five yards beyond the pin.

"Think about the ultimate penultimate categories," Ned said, "that glass of wine, is it an ultimate or penultimate solution to a hard day?"

Tyler nodded as they walked toward Ned's ball. "No doubt its penultimate. It's not really going to solve a problem. I'd think any ultimate solution would need to solve the problem."

"That's right," Ned said, "but consider how people often treat that glass of wine. Do they treat it as ultimate or penultimate?"

"I see where you're going," Tyler said as Ned set his bag down. "Problems multiply rather than resolve when we take something like wine, that might be intended to relax us after a hard day, and treat it like it's ultimate, like it's really going to solve a problem."

Ned nodded as he lined up for his shot, which landed on the opposite side of the hole as Tyler's, about equal distance from the hole.

"That's right. But of course nobody thinks wine or food or even sex is going to truly solve their problems. Intellectually we know better. But when we treat them like they're the ultimate solution, that's when trouble breaks out. We're asking them to do something they're not capable of doing."

"Because we want to feel good. We want the pain of hardship to go away," Tyler said.

Ned nodded.

"So what should we do? How should we deal with life's hardships or the pain of those hardships?" Tyler asked.

"That's a big question. What do you think?"

Tyler considered his own question and finally offered, "I don't think there's any one answer to that question. Hardship is too complex."

"Maybe. And from a certain perspective I agree with you. But I'm not a fan of waving the complexity flag too soon. I think we hide behind it. Life can be hard—very hard—but hard doesn't have to mean complicated."

"How so?"

Both men pulled their putters. Tyler pulled the pin and rested it on the side of the green.

"Consider my ultimate and penultimate categories and apply them to hardship. You've heard me talk enough about it to get the basic idea. What might be ultimate in dealing with hardship and what might be penultimate?"

Tyler thought for a moment. "Alright," Tyler said, "if I have an extremely hard week, when Friday comes, I'm going to have a couple glasses of wine. They make me feel better."

"Fair enough," Ned said.

"But I know I've not solved anything. I just feel better."

"Do you feel better in an ultimate sense or a penultimate sense?"

"What you mean?"

"Do you have a deep peace that everything is going to be alright?"

Tyler didn't answer immediately. "Sometimes, maybe, but not lately. Lately it just seemed like things were on a bad trajectory."

"So that wine made you feel better on the surface, but just below the surface you still weren't sure if your work was on a good trajectory, so you didn't have depth of peace."

"That's about right."

"So how could you have done that differently? How could you have had depth of peace despite the circumstances?"

Ned lined up for his putt as Tyler considered the question. "I like how you positioned that," Tyler said as Ned's putt stopped just shy of the hole. "You said, 'despite the circumstances.'"

"Yes, that's very intentional. Remember the swing? Circumstances are going to swing back and forth. You need to have peace despite the circumstances."

Ned tapped his ball into the hole.

"So depth of peace comes by looking beyond the circumstances to something that's ultimate."

Ned nodded.

"So you might have a glass of wine to feel better," Tyler said, "but you go deeper to have true peace."

"I do."

Tyler lined up for his putt.

"In your world, you look to God. The wine doesn't give you peace. Some sort of confidence in him gives you peace."

Ned nodded as Tyler's putt ringed the hole and rolled an additional foot away from the hole.

"I don't think I look to the wine for ultimate peace. I'd like to think I know better." Tyler paused as he considered his thoughts. "My typical weekend after a hard week might be a few glasses of wine on Friday night and a long run on Saturday. Between the two, I get straightened out enough to re-engage."

"Makes sense," Ned said, "but what gives you your confidence? Your thoughts, do they grab hold of something? What keeps you from spiraling in a negative direction?"

Thoughts of recent events went through Tyler's mind. He wasn't sure he'd not spiraled in a negative direction. "I suppose I look at the challenges in front of me and chart a course. I take confidence in my experience or my team or my skills."

"That's good. I think you should take confidence in those things, but my question now should be fairly predictable."

Tyler nodded as he closed out the hole. "You'll ask if those solutions are ultimate or penultimate."

"That's right. Those are all important aspects of life that give us confidence, but I'd suggest they all have their vulnerabilities. I have a lot of life experiences that give me confidence in navigating life's circumstances, but I know my limitations. I need to lean into something qualified to be ultimate."

"How's that work?" Tyler asked.

"When I say it's not complicated, I mean it, but that doesn't mean it's easy." Ned picked up the pin and walked back toward the hole. "Essentially, I take those circumstances, and I entrust them to God. Yes, I might play a round of golf to calm my nerves.

That's good and helpful. But if I don't get my confidence from something that transcends life, I get swept away by life."

"And you snap."

"Yes. If I'm lucky, I snap."

"You want to snap?"

Ned shook his head. "No, but if I'm living a self-centered life, I'd rather snap and expose my self-centeredness than persevere in it. I don't want to live that way."

As Tyler placed his putter back in his bag he considered Ned's comments. He understood his perspective, but there was something about it that bothered him, a deep and unaddressed resistance. Ned made sense. He was wise, and Tyler liked that, but he still didn't want Ned's faith, even if he could make a case that he might need it, or at a minimum, benefit from it. As he picked up his bag, he identified the question that had hovered over the conversation but gone unaddressed.

"What you're saying, I need to reflect on it a bit more. It does raise a significant question for me, though, Ned. You make sense, but I have to be honest. I can respect your faith, but I know I don't want it. There's an arrogance in so many people who profess faith. An intolerance. I like aspects of what you're saying, but I don't think I could get past the intolerance, and I know I don't want to. I know it sounds cliché, but I prefer the 'live and let live' motto to navigating this world."

"That's good. I like that," Ned said.

The two men walked toward a ball cleaner. As they rested their bags, Tyler continued.

"I find it a bit ironic that you talk of being self-centered and that putting God at the center is the solution to being self-centered. When I see people of faith, I see a great deal of arrogance, like they think they're right and everybody else is wrong."

Tyler expected Ned to respond, but he didn't. Ned nodded again as Tyler turned back toward his bag but said nothing. The two men walked silently toward the next tee.

As they neared the tee box, Tyler noticed something. Sally was missing.

"Ned, I think I left my driver at the last tee."

Tyler then noticed Ned had already placed his bag and was standing beside the tee box with Sally in his hand. He was swinging her back and forth, clipping the top of the grass.

The Seventeenth Hole

"WHAT are you doing, Ned?"

"Playing the game, thought I'd give Suzi a try."

"That's Sally. Feel free. I'll use yours." Tyler pulled a driver from Ned's bag and stepped up to place his tee.

The seventeenth hole was a long par four with a small water hazard and a gentle bend to the south.

"Years ago I birdied this hole," Ned said. "It's evaded me ever since. The bend in the fairway is slight, but it messes with a strong drive. If you've mastered ball movement this is the hole for application."

Tyler nodded. He took a couple practice swings with Ned's driver, and then stood with a slightly adjusted stance in hopes of hugging the bend.

He nailed it.

"Not bad. I like your driver. You'll like Sally a bit better, though."

As Ned stepped up to the tee Tyler was surprised to not see Sally in his hand. He looked to the side of the tee box where Sally leaned against Ned's bag. Ned not only didn't have Sally in his hand, but he had his putter.

"What are you doing, Ned?"

Ned took a few practice swings with his putter. After placing his ball, he lined up for his drive, a line-drive that carried about fifty yards.

"You going to tell me what you're up to, or do I have to guess?"

Ned placed his putter in Tyler's bag, took Tyler's putter for himself, picked up Sally, and then walked off with his own bag swinging Sally by his side.

As they walked, Ned looked down at the club. It was well made and could clearly take a beating. He recalled an ad in a magazine where this exact club was pictured beneath the tire of a golf cart.

As they reached Ned's ball, Ned dropped three balls beside the ball he'd driven. He then pulled Tyler's putter, his own sand wedge, and a three wood—along with Sally which he was already holding.

Tyler raised his eyebrows.

Ned stepped up to his first ball, and lined up with his sand wedge. The shot arched high and landed about forty yards from them. He lined up for the second with his three wood. As expected, the shot neared the green. For his third shot, he used Tyler's putter. The shot bounced down the fairway about thirty yards. For his final shot he lined up carefully with Sally. The shot was deep but sliced painfully into a group of trees.

"This club is horrible."

Tyler shook his head. "Speak kindly, Ned. She takes offense easily."

"I don't think so." An intense look crossed Ned's face. He held Sally loosely in his hands and began what appeared to be some sort of warm-up, gently waving Sally back and forth in the air. He then twisted back like a young boy preparing to toss a twig, and sent Sally sailing down the fairway in helicopter rotations.

Tyler looked at Ned with wide eyes. He knew Sally was fine, but—

"Ned?"

"Yes."

"Why'd you do that?"

"Do what?"

"Sling Sally down the fairway."

Ned picked up his bag of clubs and looked Tyler in the eyes, "Because I wanted to. Why not?"

The two men walked down the fairway.

Tyler stopped walking. A slight grin crossed his face. He began walking again, a bit more slowly. "I get it, Ned. You're making a point about tolerance."

"Tyler, whatever you think is fine, just don't impose your beliefs on me. In my view, if there's a club I'd like to use, I use it. If I don't like it, I throw it away. And please don't impose your rules or expectations for this game on me. I live by my own convictions. If I want to drop multiple balls on every shot, I do so. If I want to play the whole course with my putter—or your putter or that ridiculous driver—I do so. If you don't like it, that's fine. Just don't be so arrogant—and judgmental—as to impose your views on me."

"You are one of a kind, Ned Peterson."

They walked in silence. Tyler picked up Sally along the way and considered Ned's actions. The man had guts. He had to admire that. He'd never known a church guy who'd sling another man's driver down the fairway to make a point.

Tyler walked and thought as Ned picked up the balls hit by the putter and the sand wedge.

"I get it. And you make a point," Tyler finally said, "but I stand my ground, I refuse to become intolerant of other people's views."

"Who said anything about becoming intolerant?"

"You clearly don't agree with me."

"True, I don't agree we can make up our own truths, but that's not a license for high-minded arrogance. You're making an assumption and lumping two things together. I don't have all the answers, and no doubt I'm wrong about many things. We're all learning. I learn a great deal by listening to people with different convictions. In that sense, I believe very deeply in tolerance. I believe very deeply in respecting other people's views. But it's just not that simple."

Tyler appreciated the older man's humility. "What do you mean?"

Ned looked at Tyler's golf bag. "Should you be tolerant of my treatment of Sally? Should you be tolerant of suicide bombers? You said, 'live and let live.' I don't think you really believe that."

Tyler considered Ned's comments as he neared his ball. He was well-placed to make it on the green, which he did with his seven iron.

Tyler spoke up, "Those are pretty extreme examples. Aren't you overstating the case?"

Ned thought for a moment. "Fair question. Let me answer

like this. Let's create a slightly different scenario to what we just experienced."

Their walk slowed.

"Let's say you own this golf course. Let's say years ago you bought this beautifully wooded land, hired professional designers, invested several million dollars, and after years of dreaming, you owned your very own golf course."

Tyler pulled his putter.

"Let's say, then, that you open the course to the public. Word gets out. That new golf course people have seen emerging from the woods is open for play, and the owner is allowing people to play on it for free. Opening day, many people come. Over time, many more people come. After about a month, there's a constant flow of people enjoying your golf course, and you couldn't be more pleased. That is, until, you decide to take a closer look."

Ned set his bag down, pulled his nine iron, and walked to the ball he'd previously hit with the three wood.

"As you tour the course you're shocked by what you see. On the first tee, a group of teenagers are lined up on opposite ends of the first fairway driving balls at each other. Evidently, they've created their own game. You look a little further down the way, and a man is chasing his wife down the second fairway with his driver in his hand taking swings at her. You look a little further and at the third tee there's a foursome, but they're not playing golf. Instead, they've replaced their golf clubs with fishing poles. One of them has accidentally hooked one of the geese in the water hazard. You keep going and on the next fairway you find a group of people playing golf, but they're completely naked, and they've redesigned the course for themselves. From the fourth tee, they're driving for the eighth green. You go a little further, and there's a volleyball game, a softball game, and a game of cricket being played, all on your beloved golf course. You finally find two people playing a legitimate game of golf on the sixteenth fairway, but they're having a miserable experience due to all the chaos around them."

Ned lined up for his shot. His ball rolled past the pin and down the gentle slope toward the right of the green.

"Ultimately, you round everybody up, bring them to the clubhouse, insist the unclothed cover themselves, and you then begin to talk. You explain, in no uncertain terms, that this is a golf course. You dreamed it up and created it so they could all enjoy it—for free—but this did not mean they could do whatever they want on the course. To your surprise, they don't get it. Matter of fact, they call you arrogant and narrow minded. Who are you to tell them what they can and cannot do on *this* golf course. '*This* golf course?' you say. 'It's not *this* golf course. It's *my* golf course,' you gently but firmly explain. You're not trying to be possessive. You've never been possessive. You've been exceedingly generous. But you created your golf course for a purpose, with a vision in mind, and they're completely ignoring what you've intended. They don't like your words—despite your kindness and generosity. They all agree that maybe the guy swinging the driver at his wife should go, and maybe the teenagers driving balls at each other, but the rest of them aren't convinced they're doing any harm. What's the big deal if they decide to ignore your intentions and do things their own way?"

Ned paused.

"So here's my question, Tyler. I realize my description is a bit unlikely on a golf course. But let's say it's less extreme. Let's say you do have a golf course and you find the teenagers hitting balls at each other. What would you do?

After a few moments of reflection, Tyler said, "I suppose I'd kick them off the course."

Ned nodded as he placed his bag just outside the fringe and pulled his putter. "That sounds terribly judgmental of you."

Ned walked to his ball, lined up for his putt, and sent his ball about three feet from the hole.

"Tyler, I want you to consider a question. You don't have to subscribe to it, but hear me out on this. What if this world, and everything in it, is effectively God's golf course? He dreamed it up, he created it, he invested heavily in it just like you invested in your golf course. Now look around the world and consider how humanity is living. The examples I gave for your golf course are mild compared to what we're experiencing in this world. People are warring with each other on God's golf course. They're literally killing each other. Other people, they're reveling in all the goodness of God's golf course, but all the while, they're ignoring and belittling the owner of the course—even after he's allowed them to play on his course for free. Nobody earned this life. Life is a gift. We all get to play a round or two, and at a minimum, we should honor and appreciate the one who gives us this course for free. But by and large, we don't do that. We not only belittle the owner of the golf course, but we ignore his intentions for it. We make up our own rules for living, claiming we have a right to do whatever we want to do. But if this question is in fact reality, then we don't have a right to do whatever we want to do. The one who created and built the golf course has the right to create an existence on his golf course that fulfills his dream for it. It's his course. He can do that."

Tyler lined up for his putt as he considered Ned's words. His shot ringed the hole and rolled in the opposite direction of Ned's.

"So in this scenario you've created," Tyler said, "I'm the owner

of the golf course, so let's say I do have the right to kick people off
the course. I can buy that. But let's play out the scenario more
fully. I'm not talking about the owner of the golf course kicking
people off. I'm talking about the judgmental spirit of other players
on the course. When I said the intolerance of your faith offends
me, I was talking more about people than God."

"That's good, Tyler. I like that. And you make a great point.
Let's say I'm out on your golf course. And let's say I'm dialed into
your desires. If I walk around the course kicking people off, I'm
dangerously out of line. That's not at all my place. I'm not the
owner of the course, so I have absolutely no right to exercise an
authority I don't have. Scripture teaches against judging others.
When people profess to follow God, but then walk around effectively kicking people off God's course, this is both wrong and offensive, and I completely agree with you. What I do think a person might do on that golf course, though, is help people. What
if I came alongside those teenagers who were driving balls at each
other and mentored them in the game of golf. Is that being judgmental and intolerant? I don't think so. It's a completely different
spirit. I'm coming alongside a group of people—in love—trying
to help them discover the joy of the game. As I do this, no doubt
two or three of them will hurl insults at me, tell me I'm being judgmental, and order me out of their lives. If my spirit truly is one of
love, then I'm being misunderstood and mislabeled."

Both men sank their putts in silence. Tyler considered Ned's
comment but had a growing question. He could see Ned's point,
but something about it still bothered him.

As they walked toward their bags Ned said, "One more important thought about being judgmental and intolerant. If I'm out
there walking the course, and I come alongside those teenagers,

one of the primary reasons I'm gentle and respectful of them, rather than judgmental and intolerant, is because I'm fully aware of how I myself have been just like them in other areas or other seasons of my life. One of the key reasons being judgmental and intolerant is so offensive is that we all know our own propensity toward damage we've done on the golf course. If I come alongside somebody, I'm fully aware that I, too, deserve to be kicked off the course from my own mishaps."

"None of us are perfect," Tyler affirmed.

"That's correct. And we'd all do well to remember that and treat people with great amounts of humility and tolerance with that in mind."

The two men walked in silence as they neared the next tee. As they set their bags down by the tee box, Ned asked a question.

"Tyler, you said people of faith are often arrogant, and sadly, that's often true, especially those most vocal. But let me ask you a question. In that scenario I just described, where do you see arrogance?"

Tyler pulled his driver.

"I think I see your point. The people on the course, ignoring my wishes, they are, in a sense, being arrogant."

"Hear that very carefully. It takes us back to the swing. When we are self-centered, we make our own rules for living. That's arrogance. The humble look to their Creator and ask, '*What's the best way to do this?*' Arrogance is when we ignore the Creator, convinced we know better how to live this life. Humility is when we slow our lives down and listen for God's guidance. The lack of this is creating a dangerous degree of chaos in our culture. Consider the lack of ethics we've all seen in business. How much of this is people attempting their own rules of morality? And it's not just businesses, I might add. There's been a great deal of corruption, even in the church, due to these very same forces. And know that I get it. One of the more frustrating aspects of what I do is the association it carries with a loud-mouthed arrogance clothed in the faith I profess. If I were you, I wouldn't want to profess a faith in any way associated with that. Every movement has its loud-mouths and charlatans. And every movement is often misunderstood. In recent decades, maybe a good part of your life, my faith has been very misunderstood, even by those who profess it."

"But you don't want to ditch it. You came back to it."

"I did. Just like you'll take another job or start another business, despite the Tom Phelps of the world. You don't ditch the good just because there's a group of people out there who make it challenging or misrepresent you."

"It's the old adage, 'Don't throw the baby out with the bathwater,'" Tyler said.

Ned nodded.

"I hear what you're saying," Tyler said. "There's something about it all, though." Tyler paused. "I'm not sure how to articulate it. I get your logic. It just seems like there's more to it than logic. There's something in my gut that's resistant to what you're saying. I get it, but something's missing."

"That's good. Lean into that," Ned said.

"You know those people in your scenario, the ones out on the golf course doing all sorts of crazy things?"

Tyler looked toward Ned.

"Those are my people," Tyler said.

Ned smiled.

"I have a confession, Ned."

Tyler paused and smiled.

"You know that group you mentioned playing naked? I've actually done that."

Ned laughed and shook his head. "Why does that not surprise me?"

"Your illustration makes a lot of sense, but I'm not so sure those people living it up on that golf course aren't having a better time than those insisting we just play a round of golf."

"I love it."

"Love what?"

"Your observation. It's profound."

"What's my observation?"

"You're observing the people living it up on your golf course, and wondering if they're living better than if they'd embraced the game as initially intended."

"Yes, something like that," Tyler said.

"I get it, Tyler, I really do. There's a freedom to what they're doing on your golf course."

"Yes, they're living unrestricted lives. The stuffy golf course enforcer might be right—technically speaking—but I think I'd rather live free. In your words, I get the purpose and protection corners and how your perspective might work well there. I'm entirely unconvinced when it comes to the pleasure corner."

"That's good, Tyler, very good. Don't let go of that. Pleasure is critical. It's not an extra in life. If what I'm saying is good for protection and purpose, but bad for pleasure, then I'm off. All three corners need fulfillment."

Ned pulled his driver.

"Let's do something," Ned said. "Let's not dodge it. Let's apply what I'm saying to one of life's greatest pleasures."

Tyler raised his eyebrows.

"Let's talk about sex. This will be interesting."

The sex talk with a minister who happened to be the grandfather of his potential next date. Tyler wasn't sure "interesting" is the word he'd use to describe his anticipation.

The Eighteenth Hole

NEITHER man spoke as they eyed the eighteenth fairway, a long par five. Tyler placed his ball and looked toward the unseen green. His drive was long enough to land where the fairway bent slightly to the left.

Ned's drive rolled to a stop near Tyler's. The two men picked up their bags and began to walk.

"So what do you think? Sex. Ultimate or penultimate?"

Tyler appreciated Ned's direct approach.

"Based on previous criteria," Tyler said, "I'd say penultimate, but I can't imagine how a relationship with God could be better than sex. Not sure how you're going to dig your way out of that one."

"I'm not going to dig my way out of anything. Why would you say sex is a secondary pleasure?"

"Because you've been reserving the ultimate category for something that won't be subject to the law of diminishing returns, something lasting."

"And sex is susceptible to the law of diminishing returns?"

Tyler considered the question. He wasn't sure how forthright he really wanted to be with Tracy's grandfather, even if nothing ever came of it.

"Yes, sex is subject to the law of diminishing returns. As much as I hate to admit it, sex is better when there's at least a degree of moderation."

"That's good. Why do you say that?"

"Take it to an extreme," Tyler said, "A couple engages in sex three times a day. At some point, it's not as satisfying as the couple who engages sex less frequently."

"That's good. I can buy that. So if sex isn't ultimate, what is?"

Tyler looked toward a group of birds breaking from a tree.

"I honestly don't know," Tyler finally answered, "but I can't see how God could be my ultimate pleasure. That just doesn't line up. I get pleasure from many things. A business win gives pleasure. Friendships give pleasure. I feel pleasure when I exercise, drink coffee, laugh with friends. All of them bring pleasure, but I wouldn't say any of them are limitless. They all have their limits."

"Do you treat them as if they have limits?"

Ned pulled his three wood as the two of them walked toward his next shot.

"I suppose I've recognized all of these pleasures have their limitations. I don't know how much that's impacted my actions. I'd need to reflect on that a bit more. If this were a debate, I wouldn't say much more than that. But since we're talking openly, I'd say you're getting close to that realization I had back at Santorini when I said, 'This isn't it.' I've said or felt that same reality in other circumstances. I just still don't see how God could solve any of that. I'll readily admit I'm uncertain as to what will ultimately satisfy me. I just seriously doubt it's God."

"And let me say, I simultaneously agree and disagree with that statement. I don't think God will satisfy it, and yet, I do think God will satisfy it."

"I'm beginning to expect answers like that from you."

"Track with a thought," Ned said. "It will seem a little odd at first, but I think you'll get it."

Let's say you've got a lamp. It's a nice well-designed lamp with a light bulb in the socket. It's ready to go."

Tyler nodded.

"That lamp, until it's plugged in, isn't whole. It's missing something. You take that lamp, though, you plug it in, and in that moment it experiences a depth of satisfaction it's never experienced before. If the lamp could talk, it would express its pleasure of being whole, being complete, being and doing what it was made to do."

"Is that pleasure or purpose?"

"Good question. One that's best answered not with the lamp but with reality. When I finally authentically connected with God, it touched both pleasure and purpose, but the word pleasure is almost inadequate. I'd call it satisfaction. It wasn't like a buzz I knew would wear off. It was like I was whole, like I had connected to my Creator in a way I was designed to connect. There's a depth of satisfaction in that connection—that falls clearly in the pleasure corner—that has been liberating."

"Why liberating?"

Ned didn't answer as he rested his bag and lined up for his shot. His ball arched high and landed shy of the green by twenty yards.

"When I finally discovered what gives primary satisfaction," Ned said as he lifted his bag, "I no longer needed to grope after those things that give secondary satisfaction in hopes they'd do more than they're capable of doing. I could let them be what they are and enjoy them for what they are. I no longer had to strive and grope for more. It was good and profound, but I also don't want to overstate it."

"How so?"

"This is important. Experiencing God touched something deep that felt ultimate, but I've only experienced a taste of the satisfaction. I've not experienced it fully."

"What do you mean?"

"Parallels abound. Take food. You get a taste of a good meal. You can tell you're going to like it, but you haven't had the full meal yet. Or a lover kisses her significant other on the cheek. It's a taste. It's satisfying but not complete. You get the idea. When a person connects to their Creator, it's deeply satisfying. That person knows they've discovered ultimate satisfaction, but Scripture describes our experience with God as a down payment. Full payment is coming."

Tyler placed his bag, pulled his three iron, and walked to the side of his ball.

"I have a name for this condition," Ned said. "I call it *contented discontentment*."

"Interesting. Sounds self-contradictory, though."

"Maybe, but it's been quite helpful. Contented discontentment is the engaged couple. They long for each other—so they're discontent—but they're content in their discontentment, because they know their wedding day is coming."

Tyler's shot grazed the side of the fairway, nearly hitting a large elm, and then landed in a sand trap to left of the green.

"Or it's the person who's hungry, knows dinner is coming, but has to wait the fifteen minutes for it to be ready. That's contented discontentment. There's a profound difference between hunger that knows a meal is coming and hunger with no hope for a meal. I realize it sounds a bit odd, but contented discontentment has been liberating on a number of fronts."

"Why would you say it's liberating?" Tyler lifted his bag and the two men walked toward the green.

"At least two reasons. The first is that I have a very real and very deep satisfaction—right now—by walking with my Creator. I carry with me a contentment that's very deep and very profound."

"But it's not yet complete?" Tyler finished the thought.

"That's correct, which when more fully understood is more exciting than it is frustrating. There's anticipation in my life. Hope. Rather than being frustrated with a world that can't seem to satisfy my deepest desires, I live with anticipation of adventure. This adventure has taken surprising turns throughout my life, which only increases the sense of expectation and mystery for what happens beyond this life. Tyler, look at the wonders of this world. Can you imagine what the being who created all this must be like? I don't understand a great many things, but I do believe I experience a taste of relating to that being, and I live in anticipation of what it will be like to experience God in greater degrees in the future. It's an exciting way to live. It also helps a great deal with self-control."

"That's odd. You just jumped from the deep mystery of an eternal adventure to self-control. Explain that."

"Yes, that can sound like a leap, but it isn't. Consider that glass of wine you know is just past the law of diminishing returns. When you know the next drink won't satisfy you, but you also know where full satisfaction will ultimately come from, you're liberated from over-indulgence. The same can be said of over-working or over-eating or obsessing over sex. Contented discontentment has liberated me because not only do I know over-indulgence won't satisfy me, but I've tasted depth of satisfaction and am convinced full satisfaction is coming."

"So let's go back to my people on my golf course," Tyler said. "I'm supposed to tell them they will have greater pleasure by restricting their liberated living and following your God? I've done a lot of selling in my work, but that sounds like a tough sell."

"I get why you'd say that. I don't think it's a hard sell at all, though, if a person is willing to look deeply at it."

"How so?"

"Let's be forthright about sex. It's brought a great deal of pleasure in this world—like pretty much nothing else can—but it's also brought a great deal of pain. People experience abuse. They get used. They get treated like objects to be easily discarded rather than something of great value. The kind of sex you're talking about might make for an exhilarating Friday night—I'll grant you that—but I'd suggest that quite often it's associated with a great deal of pain. And I'd say this not just about sex but about a host of other things as well."

"Like what?"

Ned thought for a moment. "Let's take work and money. Someone on that golf course of yours—living what might appear to be a liberated life—is living full throttle for money. They want to accumulate great amounts of cash. And I can't blame them. I'd much prefer more money to less money. And from a certain vantage point, if they get a few business wins they're going to experience the pleasure that money provides. But they're also going to experience the frustration of more never being enough. They may appear liberated when in fact they're enslaved. They're enslaved to more. Far wealthier—and far more liberated—is the person who has the depth of insight to gain contentment with what she or he has rather than a constant groping for more. The only way I've discovered to gain true contentment is by what I just described."

"Contended discontentment," Tyler said.

"That's right. And I know that sounds odd, but it's as honest of a description as I can give. When I finally discovered where my ultimate contentment came from, I didn't have to obsess over the next deal in hopes that it would deliver something the last deal didn't."

Tyler didn't comment as Ned pulled his pitching wedge and walked to the side of his ball. Ned's shot bounced on the green and rolled to the right of the pin by about fifteen yards. As Tyler walked toward the sand trap, he wondered about Blake. How would this conversation have gone had Blake been here today?

"Ned, I have a question for you," Tyler said as he stepped into the sand trap. "Our mutual friend Blake, whom you've never actually met, is frustrated with his medical practice. It's an odd thing to me. He makes great money. He helps people. I get why he's frustrated with healthcare and all he has to do to maintain that. But his dream is unfulfilled. As I mentioned earlier, he was with us years ago when Doug asked what we wanted to make of our lives. Blake wanted to be a doctor in a third world country."

Tyler paused as he lined up for his shot. His ball rolled past the pin.

"What would you say to that? Should Blake fold up his practice and re-establish himself in a scenario where the needs are more glaring?"

Ned walked across the green toward the pin.

"What do you think?" Ned finally asked.

"I suspected you'd say that."

Ned set the pin on the fringe of the green as Tyler placed a ball marker and moved his ball out of Ned's way.

"For years, I've wished he'd do it. He's talked about it so long, I've just wished he'd go for it. What's the worst thing that could happen? He lives his dream for a few years, helps a bunch of people, and determines he misses home and comes back. He's a gifted doctor. He'd be fine."

"Not a bad plan," Ned said.

"Something tells me you'd say more than that, though."

"Why do you say that?"

"Because after nearly eighteen holes, I think I'm getting to know you."

Ned smiled. "I'd never want to discourage someone from doing something bold for the good of others, but my encouragement to a guy like Blake wouldn't be all that different than how I've encouraged you to approach your next job."

"What do you mean?"

"I encouraged you to consider your form before dropping another ball. I've seen it happen countless times. A person thinks they'll be more satisfied by switching to another career or the same career in a different setting. There are times this is highly appropriate, but there are other times the person is bringing their discontentment with them. In Blake's case, I see strong potential for a number of problems that I'd encourage him to think through. Once he thought those through, I'd love to see him make a bold move like what you've described."

"Like what? What would you have him think through?"

Ned lined up for his putt. He missed the hole by a couple of inches; his ball rolling a few feet past the hole.

"Here's the glaring problem people often miss when they seek to do something more meaningful in life. If they're doing it to satisfy their own discontentment, then they're not truly serving others, they're serving themselves. This might be the most important aspect of contented discontentment."

"How so?"

"Think about it? How might contented discontentment help a person no longer think about themselves but genuinely consider the well-being of others?"

Tyler was silent as he placed his ball and picked up his ball marker. His putt rolled to the edge of the hole and stopped.

"When people know where ultimate contentment will come from," Tyler tapped his final putt into the hole, "they no longer have to extract ultimate fulfillment from others."

"You got it. You don't have to extract ultimate fulfillment from others, and that act of extraction will be futile if you try. If a guy like Blake packs his medical bags for a third world country, but is effectively using that experience to satisfy something in him that the experience is incapable of satisfying, there will come a day he'll be disillusioned with it. My hope would be that he'd fully embrace where ultimate satisfaction truly comes from so he'd then be liberated to serve selflessly. He could more fully think about the people he's serving and not be so concerned with his own fulfillment."

"But wouldn't serving people like that be fulfilling? Seems like there's nothing wrong with that."

"Absolutely. You have to keep my ultimate and penultimate distinction in mind. Serving people is deeply satisfying. If Blake did this, he'd experience a great deal of satisfaction. But if he's hoping it would deliver ultimate satisfaction, in time, he'll find it wanting. And I've actually seen this very thing happen with those serving in third world countries. They start out with a tremendous sense of purpose. In time, though, they have a low but growing sense of frustration. It might sound unreasonable from our vantage point, but when you're in the middle of a broken system— like a third world country—in time you start to see things you wish people would fix but don't. Compassion and that deep sense of purpose are slowly replaced by frustration."

Ned's putt dropped in the hole. Tyler, already holding the pin in his hand, pulled the balls out of the hole and replaced the pin. The two men walked to their respective bags and met back at the path leading to the clubhouse.

"Ned, if it weren't for your stunt on the seventeenth hole, you might have won today. No matter, though, I'm buying if you'd like to join me for a drink at the clubhouse."

"I'd like to, but Tracy is due here shortly, and my wife is waiting for us both back home."

Tyler nodded as the two men walked side by side. "Ned, do you do counseling? Could I meet with you? I'd be willing to pay."

Ned's response was slow. He thought for a moment. "I don't do counseling. I don't take money. I do play golf, drink coffee, and eat lunch. That aside, though, let me give you a little early encouragement."

"How so?"

Ned stopped walking and placed his bag on the side of the path. "Let me see your wallet again."

Tyler set down his bag and reached for his wallet. "Here you go."

Ned opened it, pulled all the cards, and slowly rifled through them.

"Here it is." Ned stopped and held up Tyler's membership card to a local gym.

"My gym card?"

"Yes. Question for you. When was the last time you used this?"

"You heard my story. My life's been all about work. It's been a while."

"How long? Weeks or months."

"Months."

"Interesting thing about these cards. In order to get this card, you had to give them a card. You gave them a credit card, and they gave you a membership card. Is that right?"

"Something like that."

"That's what's interesting about these cards. It doesn't matter if you use the card they gave you. They'll still use the card you gave them. Every month, usage or no usage, you're charged your membership fee. You're their ideal client. You cost them nothing. Their business thrives on people signing up, getting their cards, and not using them."

Tyler nodded.

"Here's reality. People treat matters of faith similarly. They invest just enough to get their metaphorical card. Maybe they join a church, or they hang out with a guy like me every now and then. They get their card, their self-justification, but they don't use it, they don't invest their time and energy enough to truly experience life change. So no, I don't charge, but that doesn't mean our conversations won't cost you."

"How's that?"

"It'll cost you time. It'll cost you energy. And yes, if you experience life change, your heart will be different, and one day you'll want to give financially. But here's the deal. I'll talk with you, play golf with you, drink coffee with you, take you to lunch, and even buy your lunch. But for it to be meaningful, you've got to invest time and energy. If you've heard enough to know you need to dig deeper, then I'll gladly point you in a direction. Matter of fact, I've got an experience I designed exactly for that purpose. But if you blow it off enough to ward off life change, while entertaining it just enough to keep your card, then the entire exercise is useless and a waste of time."

Ned handed Tyler his wallet.

"That's fair. What's the experience?"

"I call it the *Twenty-One Day Challenge*. For twenty-one days, three weeks, my challenge to you will be to live as if what I've told you is true."

Tyler raised his eyebrows.

"You're going to have questions, good questions. And there's a great deal we've not discussed. My encouragement, though, would be a bit like I would encourage a person considering whether or not they should sit in a chair, as simple as that sounds. I can explain why the chair is comfortable and how it's sturdy enough to hold them. They can study the chair and decide for themselves what they think, and they should do that. My encouragement to a guy like you would be that you ask those questions, but also that you simply sit in the chair and see what you think. For three weeks, you embrace what I've said as true, even if you have legitimate questions about it, and see what you experience."

"I might consider that."

"Years ago I put together a twenty-one day guide. Now with the Internet, I have it posted so you can download it and follow it day by day."

Ned pulled out the scorecard, scribbled www.soultribe.tv/21 on it, and handed it to Tyler.

"You'll find it there. It will give you more context to what we've talked about and will give you guidance on how to do the Twenty-One Day Challenge."

"And after the twenty-one days?"

Ned looked toward Tyler, "I'll either hear back from you, or I won't."

As they neared the clubhouse, Tyler wondered about Tracy.

"Ned, I have an idea."

Ned looked toward Tyler.

"We never answered Tracy's question. She asked if you thought I should have coffee with her?"

"You're right. We didn't."

"Here's my suspicion. We might get along well, but she's a deeper person than me."

"I don't at all mean this negatively toward you. I like you. I really do. But you're probably right about that. When I said this was 'interesting,' though, I said that because she's been internalizing much of what we've talked about today."

Tyler looked toward the clubhouse and back toward Ned.

"I'll tell you what. Could you tell Tracy that I'm going to do your twenty-one day challenge. If after twenty-one days, I think there's something to what you're telling me, I'll get in contact with you and with her. If after twenty-one days, I'm unconvinced, or if I flake out, then I'll not waste either of your time."

Ned rested his bag on the ground.

"I like that. She will as well."

"If it's alright with you, Ned, I'm going to head back around the other side of the clubhouse. If you'd pass that along to Tracy, I'd greatly appreciate it."

Ned extended his hand, "It's been a pleasure Dr. Hill."

"Yes it has, Reverend Peterson."

Lola's

"**Y**OU have got to be kidding me!" Angie could barely contain herself. "You have repeated run-ins with her, you get her number, you don't call her for six months or nine months, you're not sure how long. Then there's this *amazing* turn of events. You wind up playing golf with her grandfather, who thinks you're somebody else, he figures it out, she turns up, and you *still*—I can barely believe this—you *still* haven't called her!"

Tyler nodded as he set his drink down.

"I'm not sure if I should respect your self-control or kick you for stringing this poor girl along!"

"I like the part where you ducked around the back of the clubhouse so you wouldn't run into her. Nice move." Doug said.

"You don't understand."

"Explain it to me!" Angie said.

"I wasn't playing a game or trying to appear uninterested. It was different than that."

Angie looked carefully at Tyler, "You really like this girl."

"I don't know her, so I don't know if I like her or not. But the reason I didn't call, and the reason I ducked around back, it hasn't been because I'm playing games. It's been something more significant than that."

Blake finally spoke, "You don't want to ruin it."

"That's it," Tyler said.

Angie looked directly at Tyler, taking it all in with a rare pause before talking, "I can respect that," she finally said, "and I suspect she will as well. Just don't wait too long. Women like a guy with depth, but you press that too far, and rather than admire your self-control, she'll be exasperated by your lack of follow through. I don't know this girl, but I think I like her for you."

"So this Ned guy really got you thinking," Blake said.

"Nobody is more surprised by that than me."

"I'm not surprised," Angie said.

"Me neither," Doug said. "The political activist in me has a list of questions, and I don't know what I think of this triangle you just explained to us. But it sounds like this guy has some sort of genuine spirituality to him. I like that." Doug took a drink. "Just don't go weird on us."

Tyler smiled, "No worries there."

"You know, as a doctor," Blake said, "there are a host of questions I'd have for a guy like Ned, but I think there's something admirable about this challenge he gave you."

"How so?" Angie asked.

"People go round and round with questions about God. I had a friend in med school who talked a lot about his faith. We'd get in pretty heated debates about it all. He never convinced me, but I heard enough to at least respect his view. What he didn't do, though, was suggest I could do something akin to what we did in the science lab throughout college."

"Form a hypothesis and test it with experimentation," Doug finished Blake's thought.

Blake nodded. "I'm not suggesting this experiment would be objective and verifiable like a science lab. Your experience will be highly subjective. But I still like it. Instead of going round and round chasing questions we all like to throw at faith, he simply asked you to try it on for a few weeks. There's some wisdom in that."

"What day are you on?" Angie asked.

Tyler shook his head. "I'm not telling."

"Why not?" Angie asked.

"Because if I tell you, you'll ask me why I haven't called Tracy yet."

Angie's eyes widened. "You're past twenty-one days, and you still haven't called! You're killing me, Tyler!"

"Where's Jack?" Tyler asked with a smile, "the meat-eater."

"I asked him to come tonight, but he's traveling on business. Maybe next month."

"And how's the patient?" Doug asked Blake.

"The patient?" Blake looked a little confused.

"The gal you hiked with when Tyler covered for you—or I should say—attempted to cover for you."

"Meagan," Blake said, "we've been out several times now. She's great."

Doug looked at the three of them. "This is interesting. There's Jack-the-Carnivore, Meagan-the-Patient, and Tracy-the-Minister's-Granddaughter. And then there's me. I'm feeling a little lonely."

Angie nearly spoke but Doug cut her off.

"But I have an idea." Doug pulled his wallet and put a twenty dollar bill on the table. "Twenty dollars to the person whose significant other I meet first, right here, at Lola's, as soon as next month's gathering."

Tyler reached into his coat pocket and pulled out an envelope. "Here's the money you all chipped in last month. I'll add it to Doug's twenty to make it a bit more interesting."

Doug's eyes widened. "With the additional funding, let's adjust the rules a bit. Half goes to the person who first appears at Lola's with either the Carnivore, the Patient, or the Minister's Granddaughter. The other half goes to the couple who sticks together for at least six months. In the event of a tie, the money is split. In the event nobody wins, drinks will be on me."

Everyone smiled as Doug raised his glass for an apparent toast.

"And let's not think of this like a bet," Doug said. "Let's think of it like a dare. That way, Tyler will actually do it."

Everyone laughed as their glasses came together.

"To the dare," they all said in near unison.

As the glasses came back to the table, Angie reached for Tyler's phone.

"What are you doing?" Tyler asked.

Angie punched buttons on Tyler's phone just out of his view. After a few moments she handed the phone back to Tyler.

"What's this?" Tyler asked.

The phone was ringing.

Tracy's name was at the top of the screen.

"You dialed her number?!" Tyler's eyes went wide.

"Hello," they all heard from Tyler's phone as he quickly raised it to his ear.

SIX KEY INSIGHTS, THE ASSESSMENT & THE DARE

Key Insight #1 – The Desire Triangle

ONE of the great gifts of life is the gift of *desire*. We are a passionate people. We have wishes and wants. There are things we want to do, places we want to go, and experiences we want to have. It's a beautiful thing, this thing called desire.

Embedded into the essence of who we are is a desire for our personal well-being. It's a good desire, easily remembered as a desire for *protection*. Much of what we do in life is driven by this desire. We not only protect ourselves physically, but we protect ourselves financially, emotionally, relationally, and the list goes on.

We want more than protection, though. We also want *pleasure*. The drive for pleasure at times works in tension with the drive for *protection*. We want the thrill—the pleasure—of jumping out of an airplane, but we don't want to die, so we strap parachutes to our backs for protection.

The drive for *protection* and *pleasure* are complemented by a third desire. We want our lives to matter. We want to make a difference. A quick glance at any day's headlines, and we instinctively know our lives must be about more than *protection* and *pleasure*. We want a life with *purpose*. We suspect we have a unique contribution to make, even if it's at times difficult to figure out exactly what that is.

It might be overly ambitious to suggest this *Desire Triangle* maps our hearts entirely. Many of our hearts' desires, though, can be found in one of these corners.

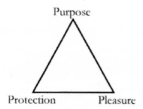

Scripture makes a piercing observation. The idea of referencing Scripture may be new, or even off-putting to you. That's fine. If you're uncomfortable viewing Scripture as if it's from God, then don't force it here. Simply hear it as ancient wisdom passed down from generation to generation for thousands of years. This particular observation is quite profound:

> Above all else, guard your heart, for everything you
> do flows from it. *Proverbs 4:23 (NIV)*

The heart—the seat of our desires—is the wellspring of life. Everything we do springs from our desires, including the activity of work. Awareness of this explains why work can be, at times, frustrating. Maybe the job isn't providing the financial resources we hoped it would. This makes us vulnerable and challenges the *protection* corner of our hearts. Maybe we're bored by endless meetings. This challenges the *pleasure* corner. Maybe we work incredibly hard but don't see why any of it matters. This challenges the *purpose* corner. If everything we do springs from our hearts, and our hearts' desires are not being met, it's no wonder we at times feel enslaved to work rather than free to fully live.

So how do we satisfy the Desire Triangle? This leads to key insight #2, or the Means of Satisfaction Triangle.

Key Insight #2 – The Means of Satisfaction Triangle

S CRIPTURE makes a complementary observation to the well-spring observation:

> And now these three remain: faith, hope, and love.
> But the greatest of these is love. *1 Corinthians 13:13*
> *(NIV)*

Boil it all down, get rid of the clutter, and according to Scripture's wisdom, there are three enduring concepts. We put our faith in something, we hope in something, and we love something. We might visualize this with a triangle complementary to the Desire Triangle.

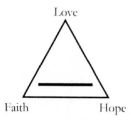

Careful thought reveals an interesting relationship between our two triangles. The first triangle represents what we want. The second triangle represents how we will get it. Take note of the line at the middle of this second triangle. This represents the object of our faith, hope, and love. The wise will ask critical questions. What will I place on this line? What will I put my faith in? What will I put my hope in? What will I love? To better understand these concepts, let's first put our jobs on this line.

We take a job, it's a good job, and we're excited about it. We might not use this language, but essentially, we put our *faith* in this opportunity to deliver a degree of *protection* in our lives. There are also aspects of the job we look forward to doing. You might say we *hope* in it. Maybe it's a leadership position, and we enjoy leading teams. Maybe it's a teaching position, and we enjoy watching the lights come on when people discover new insights. Whatever the job, part of the reason we took it was our *hope* for a degree of *pleasure* in doing it. Then there's the aspect of the job that meets a need in society. We don't typically use the word *love* to describe this, but that's exactly what it is. Our job meets a need for people—to meet a need in others is to love them—which gives us a sense of *purpose*.

Do you see it? Faith, hope, and love have an interesting relationship with protection, pleasure, and purpose. The wise will ask critical questions. What will I place on this line? What will I put my faith in? What will I put my hope in? What will I love? Those with depth of insight into their hearts will evaluate prospective candidates to fill this line by how well they satisfy the deep desires for protection, pleasure, and purpose.

Which leads us to the third key insight: the distinction between ultimate and penultimate.

Key Insight #3 – Ultimate versus Penultimate

C.S. LEWIS, Oxford professor and author of the *Chronicles of Narnia*, offered numerous insightful observations about desire. Around the time of World War II, Lewis gave a series of lectures on the radio about Christ and faith. Those lectures were later turned into a book that has captured the attention of readers for many decades now: *Mere Christianity*. In it, Lewis writes about desire. He makes a keen and profound observation very helpful here:

> Creatures are not born with desires unless satisfaction for those desires exists. A baby feels hunger: well, there is such a thing as food. A duckling wants to swim: well, there is such a thing as water.

It's a curious observation. Identify a desire and somewhere within reach you'll find satisfaction for that desire. It would be odd, Lewis suggests, if we had a desire for hunger, but there was no such thing as food, or if we had a desire for sex, but sex did not exist. Lewis then directs his thoughts to a seemingly insatiable desire, deep within us.

> If I find in myself a desire which no experience in this world can satisfy, the most probable explanation is that I was made for another world. If none of my earthly pleasures satisfy it, that does not prove that the universe is a fraud. Probably earthly pleasures were never meant to satisfy it, but only to arouse it, to suggest the real thing.

His point? There is a deep hunger, a deep thirst, a deep desire seemingly nothing in this world can satisfy. We can attempt to satisfy that desire, but search this world, high and low, and that deep desire will maintain its hunger. What then? Real living, profound living, deep living, Lewis would tell us, transcends this world. We live in a temporal world, but we are not temporal people. We are eternal. If we are eternal, then temporal satisfactions will not be enough. We need an eternal satisfaction for our deepest desires.

Countless things in life deliver protection, pleasure, and purpose. A marriage, for example, delivers a degree of each. Protection is given by the two people working together to carve out a life for themselves. Pleasure is given by the two people enjoying each other's company and intimacy. Purpose is given by their mutual vision of what they hope to accomplish together, and possibly by raising up a new generation. Little things in life touch one corner or another as well. Food touches both the pleasure and protection corners, and if you're the chef, a degree of purpose. Sex touches the pleasure corner and possibly the purpose corner, if there is conception. Exercise touches both protection and pleasure and gives us the strength we need to fulfill our purpose. The list is seemingly endless for potential objects of our faith, hope, and love to deliver satisfaction to protection, pleasure, and purpose.

But the wise among us recognize the limited capacity of most everything on the list. Yes, marriage can deliver degrees of protection, pleasure, and purpose, but our hearts will still yearn for other things in life, and maybe yearn a great deal if the marriage goes south. Food is a wonderful gift in life, but as satisfying as a good meal can be, none of us expect that meal to be the ultimate satisfaction of our lives. Sex, too, has its limitations, although some seem to hope otherwise. Name just about anything—travel, nutrition, friendship—these all deliver degrees of satisfaction in one or all of the corners, but none of us look to these and think, "That's all I need in life. It's my ultimate satisfaction." At least, that's not what we say. Unfortunately, it is how we treat many things, and work is no exception.

But what if we didn't? What if we recognized that work— along with marriage, food, sex, exercise, travel, adventure, and more—is designed to be penultimate but not ultimate. We can and should expect work to deliver a degree of satisfaction, ideally to each of the corners, but what if we didn't expect work to deliver ultimate satisfaction? There's something profound and important in this, maybe even liberating, but how do we do it? Certainly awareness goes a long way, but awareness doesn't solve the deep reality of our very hungry hearts. These deep desires of protection, pleasure, and purpose are not trivial desires. They're powerful. They propel us through life in search of depth of satisfaction, in search of something ultimate, and take us to the fourth key insight: ultimate satisfaction.

Key Insight #4 –
Ultimate Satisfaction

I N the middle of Scripture is a collection of writings—poems really—called the Psalms. Unlike any other portion of Scripture, the Psalms are an outpouring of the heart. On one page, the writer cries out in agony over disappointment and disillusionment. Turn the page and you find celebration, dancing, and song. Open the Psalms and you will find yourself in them. They are highly representative of the ups and downs of daily living.

In one such Psalm we read:

> The sorrows of those will increase who run after other gods. *Psalm 16:4 (NIV)*

The importance of this statement is missed when we limit our thinking to what we traditionally think of as "gods." We might paraphrase this statement by saying:

> The sorrows of those will increase who treat penultimate means of satisfaction as if they are ultimate.

When we look to our work as if it is our means of ultimate satisfaction, we are giving our work god-like status. Scripture describes this as a path of increasing sorrow. Why? Because our work will not live up to the expectations we place upon it. The same could be said of any other means for satisfaction better fit for the penultimate list. Marriage and parenting can be tremendously fulfilling but are dangerously disappointing if we expect them to be ultimate. Food and drink are wonderful gifts, but treat them as ultimate, and addictions are born. Adventure and thrills make life exciting, but if we put them on the ultimate line, in time the buzz wears off, and we're left still searching for more.

But what happens when we let God be ultimate? The previously mentioned words of C.S. Lewis come echoing back here. "*If I find in myself a desire which no experience in this world can satisfy, the most probable explanation is that I was made for another world.*" If nothing in this world can fully satisfy my deep desires for protection, pleasure, and purpose, maybe this is by design. Maybe this deep and insatiable desire was put there to cause us to seek out that which is ultimate and not be satisfied with temporary solutions. When they asked Jesus to name the most important command in all of Scripture, he cited the command to love God with all our heart, soul, mind, and strength. What if we read this command like an instruction manual to our hearts: "*Here is how you care for your heart. Your heart is insatiably hungry, so don't expect it to be satisfied with something small. Let your heart feast upon that which is ultimate. If you want to care for your heart, let it love God with everything it has."*

It's a fascinating thought, but let's not embrace it too quickly. Let's ask if this will really work. If we love God and let him be ultimate, will the clouds part, will we be finally and fully satisfied? Some seem to suggest this, but it misses the big picture and cheapens reality. It's here we must lean into the fifth key insight, the perspective of *contented discontentment.*

Key Insight #5 – Contented Discontentment

CONTENTED discontentment is the state of being when we know where satisfaction will come from, even though we don't fully have it. Physical hunger is in a state of contented discontentment when the meal is cooking but not quite ready. This is a very different kind of hunger from the hunger that doesn't know if it will eat today, or this week, or ever. When a person encounters God in this world, Scripture describes our relationship with God as a taste or a down payment. It's deeply satisfying, but it's not yet complete.

One of the great frustrations of life is when we take temporary solutions—jobs, sex, food, adventure—and attempt to satisfy an eternal longing. It won't work. But when we look to that which is ultimate to be our ultimate satisfaction, we get a taste of this in our current existence, and it excites expectation for what is to come. We observe the world around us. We observe the mountains, the oceans, the stars above, and the friends beside us, and when we quiet ourselves, we acknowledge a deep sense of something powerful beyond explanation that brought all of this into existence. If we listen, and if we pursue, Scripture teaches we can actually commune with this God. We're told he's not some impersonal force but a personal and powerful being who wants to know and be known, just like we do. When we taste this relationship, it is profound. So profound, there is a deep sense of our hearts finally finding their resting place. This experience, it is not yet complete, but it is real, and propels us to seek God more fully. As we walk through life and open ourselves to his presence, we increasingly experience God both powerfully and personally. Scripture states it like this:

> Come near to God and he will come near to you.
> *James 4:8 (NIV)*

Experiencing God is both powerful and personal—it's deeply profound—but it's also not yet complete. We get enough to experience depth of satisfaction, so we're content with that, but it's a discontented contentment, because we instinctively know there is more to come.

The implications of contended discontentment on our penultimate satisfactions are profound as well, which leads us to our sixth key insight.

Key Insight #6 – Freedom

WHAT happens when work no longer has to be our ultimate satisfaction? What happens when it take its rightful place as a penultimate solution to our desires? Maybe the most surprising result is that we like and appreciate work *more* not less. Why? Because no longer are we frustrated with a job that fails to deliver ultimate satisfaction. Instead, we enjoy it for what it is rather than hate it for what it's not. Many words could describe this state of being, but freedom may state it best. When work must deliver a degree of satisfaction it is incapable of delivering, we squeeze the job in such a way that we are enslaved to it. We don't just need the job, we *need* the job, and this is a miserable way to live. But when we recognize work was never intended to bring ultimate satisfaction, and when we know where ultimate satisfaction can and does come from, we can hold our jobs with open hands rather than white knuckled grips. Such living is liberating and free.

What about other penultimate objects of satisfaction? Consider relationships. What happens when friendships, marriage, or even parenting no longer have to deliver ultimate satisfaction? Here as well, maybe most surprising is that we become better friends, better spouses, and better parents. Why? Because no longer are we squeezing the life out of our relationships expecting them to be and do something they are incapable of being and doing. We've all seen or experienced parents whose entire lives revolve around their children. Kids should be a high priority, but if given god-like status in a family, nobody wins, especially the kids.

That's relationships. Consider a different category. What happens when we let life's appetites rest in penultimate positions? No longer do we look to food and drink and sex as if they are going to deliver an ultimate satisfaction they are incapable of delivering. Not only are we able to finally enjoy them for what they are, but we are also increasingly able to walk away from addictive and destructive habits and patterns. That's freedom! We can't do this if we treat them as ultimate, even if we don't use that language. When treated as ultimate, we over-eat, over-drink, and over-obsess over sexual satisfaction. Such living is destructive to ourselves and those around us.

We all work. The CEO works, the stay-at-home parent works, the activist works, the teacher works. Even the excessively wealthy work to protect their financial interests. We work so we can have a life, but we've all had this challenged. We're challenged by the over-bearing boss, or the endless demands of clients, or the non-stop demands of running a household. A helpful way to under-stand work frustration could be summed up in this simple thought: *work frustration happens when our work fails to ade-quately meet our desires for protection, pleasure, and purpose.* We put our job at the center of our faith, hope, and love, but it fails to deliver in an ultimate sense.

But what if we didn't do this? What if we let work take its good and healthy place in our lives, as a penultimate satisfaction? Rather than a white-knuckled grip on something that will leave us wanting, we live with an open-handed perspective that lets some-thing be good and important in our lives without expecting it to do something it's incapable of doing. There's liberation in this. No longer must we squeeze the life out of work, or worse, let it squeeze the life out of us. We can engage it, and engage it boldly, and we can then set it down, and embrace other aspects of life. We can do this, because we know where ultimate satisfaction comes from, and we can enjoy the taste of ultimate satisfaction available for us today.

The Assessment

L ET'S engage in a brief assessment. Knowing where we are empowers us to identify our own next steps. Let's consider three perspectives: the Spiritualist, the Secularist, and the Freebird, and let's then consider which of these is most representative of ourselves.

The Spiritualist

Spiritualists understand and embrace the *ultimate* but do so at the expense of the *penultimate*. They know and embrace what it means to put God at the center of their faith, hope, and love, and in so doing, there is a deep sense of protection, pleasure, and purpose in their lives. The challenge for the spiritualist, though, is they have neglected the daily practices that make life work.

Scripture not only teaches deep spiritual truths that bring depth of satisfaction, but there is also a great deal of practical wisdom for daily life. Consider Scripture's proverbial wisdom:

> All hard work brings a profit, but mere talk leads only to poverty. *Proverbs 14:23 (NIV)*

The spiritualist misses this. Hard work and profit are not valued, and this compromises one's life. Hard work and profit matter, and matter significantly, in a penultimate sense. When we let them take their healthy place in our lives, great good can come from our efforts.

Consider another bit of street wisdom from a writing in Scripture referred to as Ecclesiastes:

> If the ax is dull and its edge unsharpened, more strength is needed, but skill will bring success. *Ecclesiastes 10:10 (NIV)*

The point? Skill matters. Neglect your education, your development, your personal well-being, and life will be harder than it needs to be. Put your faith, hope, and love—in a penultimate sense—into becoming an expert at something, and you will have greater protection, greater pleasure, and greater purpose in life. The spiritualist must consider this exhortation carefully.

That's the spiritualist. There's another ditch, though, this one on the opposite side of the same road.

The Secularist

Secularists understand and embrace the *penultimate* but do so at the expense of the *ultimate*. They hone their skills, work hard, enjoy life's adventures, and experience life's thrills, and when done well, they increase their protection, pleasure, and purpose. The challenge for secularists, though, is they neglect the thirst of their souls. Hear carefully Scripture's description of the secularist:

> My people have committed two sins: They have forsaken me, the spring of living water, and have dug their own cisterns, broken cisterns that cannot hold water. *Jeremiah 2:13 (NIV)*

Deep within us is a thirst. It's a profound thirst designed to propel us toward the greatest of satisfactions. We were not designed to live separate from God digging out cisterns and wells incapable of satisfying an eternal thirst. Attempt this and life may have moments of thrill and wonder, but through it all will be a deep and unquenchable thirst. It may seem simple—too simple—that a connection with God could truly satisfy our deepest thirst. Jesus acknowledged this in prayer when he said, "You have hidden these things from the wise and learned, and revealed them to little children" (Matthew 11:25). A life with God at the center of our faith, hope, and love is simple enough for children, and profound enough for the thirstiest of souls.

The Freebird

At least two words describe the freebird: intentional and holistic. They are deliberate in their pursuit (intentional), and their pursuit is of both ultimate and penultimate satisfactions (holistic). The result is a liberated life. To best understand this, consider the tightrope walker.

The tightrope walker moves across a wire stretched high above the ground. This wire is their lifeline. It provides protection (by keeping them from falling to the ground), pleasure (it's a thrill to walk so high), and purpose (they provide onlookers with entertainment and awe). That wire, though, is not their ultimate protection. Stretched ten to twenty feet above the ground, almost imperceptible, is a net. This net, metaphorically speaking, is their ultimate protection, and dramatically influences their performance on the wire. Because the net is there, they are liberated and free to go for it. No longer must they cling to that wire for their lives. They don't want to fall—it's no fun to fall—but the fact that the wire is not their sole lifeline liberates and frees them to attempt feats they'd never consider without it.

Those who embrace and enjoy ultimate satisfaction by communing with God have available to them a liberated way of living. No longer must they cling to any and every penultimate solution in hopes that it will deliver the life for which they long. Yes, they are intentional—very intentional—about developing and cultivating life's penultimate solutions, but they do so in a spirit of freedom and joy, because they have realistic expectations on what these solutions can and cannot do. No longer must they squeeze the life out of a job, a relationship, or a drink. Now they are able to enjoy these gifts without imposing god-like expectations upon them. And to be sure, communion with God does much more than that net for the tightrope walker. Not only does he "catch us" so to speak, but there is a communion—a relationship—that a personal being is able to give that an inanimate net cannot. To stretch the analogy a bit farther than it should probably be stretched, it's as if the net is not just available to catch the tightrope walker, but the net is alive, talking to, coaching, and encouraging the tightrope walker. God is ultimate, but he is also available to be intimately involved in guiding us through life's penultimate realities.

In the very conversation where Jesus expressed the childlike simplicity of communing with God, he invites us to a new way of living:

> Come to me, all you who are weary and burdened, and I will give you rest. Take my yoke upon you and learn from me, for I am gentle and humble in heart, and you will find rest for your souls. For my yoke is easy and my burden is light. *Matthew 11:28-30 (NIV)*

The spiritualists weary themselves by neglecting life's penultimate opportunities and gifts. The secularists weary themselves by denying their deepest spiritual need and attempting life apart from God. Jesus comes alongside us all and beckons us to break free and experience the rest that comes from satisfied desires. No longer must we struggle and strive in search of the next fix that will make us feel whole. He is gentle and humble in heart, and through him, we find rest for our souls.

The Dare

So who are you? Are you a spiritualist, a secularist, or a free-bird? Like any spectrum of categories, no one description fits any of us perfectly, but which most reflects your reality? Self-awareness goes a long way toward determining your best next step.

If you're a spiritualist, potential next steps abound, far beyond anything that could be suggested here. Maybe you need to cultivate fun in your life. Maybe you need to hone your craft and better your life by becoming an expert at something. Maybe you need to be more intentional about finding love. Maybe you need to play more, sing more, dance more. Maybe you need to travel. There are countless penultimate satisfactions in this life. You're encouraged to find yours and take your step.

If you're a secularist, you're encouraged to consider the *Twenty-One Day Challenge*. No doubt you have questions. Good questions. You're encouraged to ask and pursue answers to your questions, but this encouragement comes with a bit of caution. Don't let your questions be a smokescreen. Ask your questions, but the invitation to pursue God is a bit like an invitation to ride on an airplane. You can look at a plane, study aeronautical engineering, quiz the pilot and the mechanics, and walk the tarmac looking for any defects. Such activities may be good and helpful, but at some point you need to simply get in the plane and let it take you up and over the clouds. You'll know minutes into your ride whether or not it was good decision. The *Twenty-One Day Challenge* is a simple way to take a ride.

If you're a freebird, no doubt you know your susceptibilities. You've made progress on both your ultimate and penultimate satisfactions, but like the rest of us, you have your vulnerabilities. Vulnerabilities in one season of life might be replaced by different vulnerabilities in another. What's your vulnerability today? What are you treating as ultimate that is penultimate? Where are you most vulnerable to do so? Maybe you're in a tough season with money or work or relationships. What's your next step with each of these? Maybe you've experienced God in your life, but in recent weeks, months, or years, your heart has grown spiritually cold, and you need to revitalize your daily communion with God. The *Twenty-One Day Challenge* might be helpful to you, but only you know you.

Whoever you are and wherever you are, whether you appreciate the thoughts in this book or think they're ridiculous, it seems appropriate to end not with a challenge, but with a dare. If we were together, sitting across the table from each other, and enjoying lively conversation, I'd ask for your next steps, and I hope you'd ask for mine. After a bit more discussion, we'd pull out our wallets and each put twenty dollars on the table. We'd raise our glasses and toast to our agreement. In the coming weeks, we'd each take our next steps. If one of us didn't, the other would take the money. If both of us did, the one who finished first would take the money. If neither of us did the work, the forty dollars would go to a charity we agreed upon. Let's not think of this like an obligation or something we should do but likely never will. Let's think of it like a dare. That way, maybe we'll actually do it.

21 day
CHALLENGE

www.soultribe.tv/21

Recommend

If you found *Freebird* helpful and would like to recommend it to your friends, you can easily send them a link to the book by going to www.soultribe.tv/freebird.

Reviews

Your reviews are greatly appreciated. Share your thoughts at www.soultribe.tv/freebird-reviews.

Thank You...

This book has been a team effort.

A special thanks to my editors—Sherilyn Villareal, Andy Meisenheimer, Carla Foote, and Pam Shoup—who each brought a unique perspective that completed this book.

My friend and mentor John Burke has been a tremendous source of encouragement and support in countless ways over the past twenty years. This book would not exist without him.

The Dig Group—Aaron Roughton, Dowd McDonald, Jeremy Ford, John Kane, and Craig Epstein—all influenced this book far more than they likely realize and gave much needed encouragement to get it done.

The strategists—Beth Jusino, Robb Overholt, and Mark Vermilion—whose thoughts and ideas on how to get this book into the hands of readers clarified the vision and inspired perseverance.

My parents—Jan Shurtz and the original Rick Shurtz—who among countless other important parental acts in my early years, made me write a paragraph every week in addition to my homework. I hated it, but for reasons I can't fully explain, I've kept writing.

My wife—Deborah Shurtz—it would take a book within itself to say all I'd want to say, but thank you. I love you very much. And a special thanks to our kids—Ellie and Chase—for making life fun and exciting. I love you both more than you will ever understand.

CPSIA information can be obtained
at www.ICGtesting.com
Printed in the USA
FFOW05n1854190815

9 780990 737902